Cooking the Gullah Way, Morning, Noon, & Night

Cooking the

Gullah Way

Morning, Noon, and Night

Sallie Ann Robinson

with Gloria J. Underwood

Foreword by JESSICA B. HARRIS
The University of North Carolina Press
Chapel Hill

All photographs by Karen M. Peluso. © 2007 Karen M. Peluso.
Designed and set in Galliard by Kimberly Bryant
Manufactured in the United States of America
The paper in this book meets the guidelines for permanence
and durability of the Committee on Production Guidelines for
Book Longevity of the Council on Library Resources.

Library of Congress Cataloging-in-Publication Data
XXXXXXXXXXXXXXXXXXXXXXXXXXXXXXXXXXXXX
XXXXXXXXXXXXXXXXXXXXXXXXXXXXXXXXXXXXXX
XXXXXXXXXXXXXXXXXXXXXXXXXXXXXXXXXXXXX
XXXXXXXXXXXXXXXXXXXXXXXXXXXXXXXXXXXXXX
XXXXXXXXXXXXXXXXXXXXXXXXXXXXXXXXXXXXX
XXXXXXXXXXXXXXXXXXXXXXXXXXXXXXXXXXXX
XXXXXXXXXXXXXXXXXXXXXXXXXXXXXXXX

ISBN 978-0-8078-3150-2 (cloth: alk. paper)
ISBN 978-0-8078-5843-1 (pbk.: alk paper)

cloth   10 09 08 07 06   5 4 3 2 1
paper   10 09 08 07 06   5 4 3 2 1

To my hero and a wonderful friend,
who has served our country in the U.S. Marines,
the Beaufort County Police Department,
and two years in Iraq:
SERGEANT EDWARD T. HARRIS

Contents

Muffins oo

    Carolina Blueberry Muffins oo
    Homemade Apple Nut Cinnamon Muffins oo
    Comeyah Banana Nut Muffins oo
    Grandmomma's Sweet Tada Muffins oo
    Gullah Bacon Corn Muffins oo
    Hearty Oatmeal Raisin Muffins oo
    Momma's Crackling Muffins oo

NOON oo

Sandwiches oo

    Fried Shrimp Sandwich with Lettuce and Tomato oo
    Fried Soft-Shell Crab Sandwich oo
    Open-Face Crabmeat Sandwich oo
    Baked or Broiled Fish Sandwich oo
    Fried Oyster Sandwich oo

Soups oo

    Grandmomma's Chicken Noodle Soup oo
    'Fuskie Seafood Gumbo oo
    Island Shrimp Creole oo
    Easy Vegetable Soup oo
    Cabbage Soup oo
    Carolina Chili oo
    Yondah Black-Eyed Pea Soup oo
    Specialties oo
    Creamy Garlic Butter Mashed Tadas oo
    Garlic Home Fries oo
    Homemade Meatballs oo
    Sallie's Seafood Spaghetti oo
    Homemade Cheese Biscuits oo
    Ham and Tada Salad oo
    Chicken Coop Egg Salad oo
    Daufuskie-Way Deviled Eggs oo

Foreword

Sallie Ann Robinson represents a link in a very long chain. A native of the Sea Islands that were, until well into the twentieth century, cultural microclimates where the traditions of times past were kept alive, she is a member of the Gullah culture that is one of black America's pivot points with the African continent. Those who have seen the films *Conrack* or *Daughters of the Dust* or who have read Pat Conroy's *The Water Is Wide* or more scholarly anthropological studies know of these islands off the Atlantic coast from Carolina to Florida. For almost a century following the Civil War, the barrier islands, known as the Sea Islands, were reachable only by boat, creating an isolation in which the descendants of the enslaved were able to maintain and guard their cultural patrimony. The result is a rich culture with a unique form of spoken English that maintains African sonorities and a tradition of praise houses where Christianity is celebrated with profound fervor yet coexists with traditional beliefs. On these islands, there is also a West African–inflected material culture that is displayed in everything from the handwoven sweetgrass baskets, which have become collector's items, to nets used for shrimping and fishing that are cast with a grace duplicating that of other fishermen across the Atlantic. Most of all, the islands maintained a way of life that honors old values of kinship and community. Sallie Ann Robinson is a member of that community. As one whose "navel cord was cut" on Daufuskie Island, she is a living witness to times past and times passed. In *Cooking the Gullah Way, Morning, Noon, and Night*, her second cookbook, she continues her saga and gives the reader an inside view of daily life in the Gullah community. In this, Robinson joins a select crowd, for the Gullah way of life is one that has rarely been documented by its own.

In the pages that follow, Robinson shows us life as it was, before the current modernization of Daufuskie, through her eyes and through her family memories. We are initiated into the ways of "beenyahs" (natives) and observe from the side as Robinson and her family go about their daily activities. We watch as Momma and Grandmomma and myriad aunts and cousins do wash and the children go about their chores. We can see the gnarled hands of her father as he patches his nets and prepares to go fishing, and we can almost taste the fresh mullet that fills the footbath when he returns with his catch. We hear her mother's admonitions and teachings and bask in the warmth of family and community.

The vignettes are evocative glimpses into a fascinating culture. But, this is, after all, a cookbook, and Sallie Ann Robinson's recipes also tell us much about the life of the community. Progressing throughout the day from morning to noon to night, the recipes allow us all to come to the table and participate in the culinary richness of the Gullah culture. Maybe we'll join her in a "day clean breakfast" plate of crispy smoked bacon and cheese grits or a slice of toast topped with prissy peach preserves, or a noontime fried shrimp sandwich with lettuce and tomato accompanied by a bowl of 'Fuskie seafood gumbo, or a local Sea Island country boil served as an evening meal. Perhaps it will be a plate of salmon stuffed with crabmeat and shrimp or a simple mug of orange peel tea served along with a pecan crunch cookie—or just a taste of 'Fuskie backyard pear wine. From their down-home names to their rich flavors, the recipes allow us all to savor Robinson's taste of Gullah culture and to recreate her world in our own.

Sallie Ann Robinson has a parting gift for us. In the final section of her book, Robinson acquaints us with the world of Gullah folk beliefs and home remedies. We learn how ailments like hiccups and indigestion were cured in the old times, and how the community dealt with such maladies as high blood pressure, pneumonia, and asthma. We are treated to a look at the how her family learned to tell when a storm was brewing and how they weathered the storms. We marvel at her mother's tenacity in keeping her family healthy and at just how the community ministered to its own needs, both physical and spiritual.

The wondrous world that Sallie Ann Robinson describes in *Cooking the Gullah Way, Morning, Noon, and Night* connects the dots for many of African descent in this country, whether Gullah or not. This is a world where the African past and the American present came together to create a new and unique culture. It is a world that has been, and still is, at serious risk, for the world that gave birth to Gullah culture has been discovered by outsiders who revel in the swoop of egrets and the sounds of the sea lapping against sand beaches. Developers are constructing gated communities, and the old ways have dwindled or died out. Bridges now connect the islands to the mainland, and much has been transformed. The Gullah culture, though, endures and has gained strength from the struggle for survival. The direct result of being at risk is a renewed interest in Gullah culture. In this, Sallie Ann Robinson is a part of the vanguard. Her recipes and reminiscences help fix a place and time when life was different, and the world seemed a simpler place. Little did she suspect, when she was one of the students that Pat Conroy celebrated in his book *The Water Is Wide*, that one day she would write history both cultural and culinary by telling the story of her Gullah home from the point of view of a "beenyah" who grew up with the smell of pluff mud in her nostrils and the taste of Gullah home cooking on her tongue. All Americans, cooks or not, are richer for her telling of it.

Jessica B. Harris

Acknowledgments

For some folks, it is a place where they were born and grew up, and then moved away from. But for others, like me, it is a place where your navel cord was cut, and your heart often wanders to the good and bad times you lived there. You have memories of being young and free, with few or no worries. My sisters and brothers and I had no concerns about where our next meal, the shoes on our feet, or the clothes on our back were coming from. Pop and Momma kept us close, and we did not take things for granted. Good behavior and manners ruled in all things that were said and done. Meals were cooked and ready mostly on time, as we all pulled together to get the work done. Later we would happily gather at the dinner table to break bread over Momma's fixin' and mixin'. No one ever left the table without a bellyful.

For years I had no clue that the small island called Daufuskie where I grew up would have such a powerful impact on my life long after I had moved away. People move away from home for all sorts of reasons, but for me it wasn't about choice. Very few natives live on Daufuskie nowadays; many live over on the mainland just a boat ride away.

Pop and Momma had strict rules but very little education. Even so, they have lived life with big hearts.

Living on Daufuskie when I was young wasn't about the color of people's skin or whether they were rich or poor. Giving and being there for one another kept the community together. Pop was a wise man who believed that "nuttin' gets done when ya lyin' in bed." We were not allowed to judge another without cleaning up our own mess first. One thing is sure: we didn't let not having hinder us. We were happy with our unique southern way of life, a way that made us strong because we earned all that we achieved in both good times and bad. We were hard working, independent, and responsible for all we had to do. We always had high standards, pride, and respect for others. Our soil was rich and natural, and we grew many fresh organic vegetables in our gardens. The woods were filled with adventure and a variety of wild game, berries, nuts, and herbs. We learned of both their goodness and danger. God gave us the stars, the moon, the sun, and the tides, as well as our changing seasons. We gave our time and labor and made it all work for us. I have memories of many moments of joy, pain, spirituality, and love, but, most of all, memories of blessings. It is the blessings that have guided me this far.

I give many thanks to all who share with me this walk down memory lane. A wonderful friend who helped with the editing of this cookbook, Gloria Underwood, deserves thanks for her patience and dedication. Special thanks to my new family members, Clinton (a poet), Karen (a photographer/poet), and Momma Peggy Campbell. I enjoy their warm and charming ways. Karen took the photographs that appear in the book. We had a lot of fun putting this together.

This book is for many special people in my life, starting with my wonderful mom, Mrs. Albertha R. Stafford, who lies on her sickbed. She loves to join in with stories and laughter as I comb and braid her hair while I pick her brain in conversations. We have enjoyed many memories as we've talked about the good times on 'Fuskie with our families and friends. It is also for my loving children: Jermaine Adonuise Robinson and his wife Kecia Renee Polite Robinson, Rakenya Niccole Robinson, Isiah Lamar Coleman and Deidre Moore, and Thomas Morris Bush.

I am so grateful for Nana's loving grands: Jaquasha, Jermaine, Charmaine, Janaesha, Tanashia, Dijana, and Isiah Lamar Coleman Jr. I offer this book in appreciation of my mother's sisters and of my 32 first cousins; many, many second and third cousins; and cousins to the end, wherever it stops. A very special thanks to my grandaunt, one of my grandfather's sisters, Amelia Jones. For the many more family members not mentioned, especially for all my siblings, with whom I had the best of times growing upon and off Daufuskie Island, and their families—I love you all. Special thanks to all the Daufuskie Island families and friends still here and those now gone; to girlfriends Cynthia Murray, from day one, and Lauretta Chisholm, to the end; and to all of those, near and far, who have become my friends as we travel through life.

Many special thanks also to my favorite author and famous teacher, Pat Conroy, and his wife, Cassandra King Conroy. I am proud to have been one of your 18 students on Daufuskie. You have touched and inspired people the world over.

I met a wonderful lady about 20 years ago, shortly after the birth of my youngest son, Thomas Bush. Many got to know of her, but I got a lesson in knowing her. Heartfelt thanks, Sarah Bush.

Introduction

My Daufuskie Gullah

My earliest memories of life on Daufuskie Island are of family and neighbors, of work and play. The women worked hard around the house; they cooked over woodstoves and made quilts. They were always fussing over us children (or "churn" as they would say). When the weather permitted, the men, young and old, cast shrimp nets in the local waters and caught all kinds of seafood for our meals. When it was too cold, they would mend their old nets, humming a favorite tune, or they would knit new ones. We kids would watch with fascination and make our own early attempts to capture these skills from the women and the men.

Even though I grew up on Daufuskie in the 1960s, these very same scenes would have been around almost 300 years earlier, when the first Africans—my Gullah ancestors—arrived on Daufuskie. Historians say the Gullah people reach as far north as the North Carolina coast and as far south as the barrier islands along the northern cost of Florida. Today, "Gullah" refers to descendants of the people from the West African rice coast who were enslaved and brought to America; it also refers to descendants of blacks who settled in southeastern coastal areas after the Emancipation Proclamation was issued in 1862.

The derivation of the word "Gullah" has been lost; however, a couple of explanations survive. It may be a shortened form of "Angola," the region from which a large number of Africans were imported to the Sea Islands. Or it may be a version of the name of a specific Liberian group or tribe called "Golas," "Goras," "Gulas," or "Golos," among other variations. "Geechee" is often used as a synonym for "Gullah." Some sources say the term "Geechee" refers to Gullah people who lived in the area of the Ogeechee River south of Savannah, Georgia. Other sources consider it a term of derision.

Like the other barrier islands, Daufuskie Island was so isolated that the Gullah heritage was able to exist there well into the second half of the twentieth century. Many of the recipes and folk cures presented here are inherited from my Gullah ancestors, as are certain skills, various beliefs and superstitions, and a number of words that have remained part of the culture on Daufuskie and the other Sea Islands.

A native's tin-roofed house near where Sallie once lived on Daufuskie Island.

A number of art forms are still practiced today, with a renewed inter-est from the younger generations. The sweetgrass baskets have become treasured objects that, useful as well as beautiful, grace tables and walls in homes not just on Daufuskie, but throughout the Lowcountry and the Sea Island area. Some artisans continue to process indigo to dye the fabric that will become scarves, dresses, and shirts or will end up in quilts. Not only do descendants of native Sea Islanders weave beautiful fabrics, they also continue the craft of creating and repairing the shrimp nets that help provide a source of income as well as sustenance. The descendants who cast for shrimp today in the local creeks perform this task with the same grace as performers in a traditional dance.

Gullah people belong to a culture that loves, worships, and praises God. Originally, many enslaved Africans brought their own God(s) with

The First Union African Baptist Church, which Sallie's family has attended for 120 years.

them from their homeland. Over time, the Europeans' God was presented to—or, in some cases, forced upon—them. One of the traditions gradually dying out is the Praise House. Every Sunday on Daufuskie, Mrs. Sarah Grant would ring the church bell, and the church would fill with people. There were always shouts of praise and rejoicing as we would sing the old songs that gave us words to live by during the coming week.

Apart from formal religion, belief in the spirit world was common on the Sea Islands. On occasion, you will see a house with the shutters around the windows and the door frames painted "haint" blue; this blue shade, according to tradition, keeps evil spirits out of the house. On Daufuskie, our daily lives were embedded with superstitions and eased by home remedies to fix what needed immediate attention until we could get to the doctor on the mainland. It is difficult today to believe that we lived that way, but it was a reality for all of us: our lives were governed by those old folktales.

The Gullah dialect is a derivative of various African tribal languages added to English, with some elements of West Indian speech thrown in. All of the Sea Islands had their own versions of Gullah dialect. A few words are recognizable to contemporary speakers of English, but many words and phrases, as well as the sentence structure, are different from European language patterns. "Ova deh" means "over there," "down yondah" is another version of "over there" or "down there," and "hole on" is a version of "hold on," as in "wait a minute." "Hona chile" is an endearment reserved for children. Other words and phrases are not so predictable: "famember" for "remember," "beenyah" as a term for an island native and "comeyah" as a term for a newcomer, "whafamadda?" for "what's wrong?" and "wayah for gwain" for "where are you going?"

Working and Playing on Daufuskie

Every day of our childhood we worked. For us it was not a way to get an allowance; it was a way of life and a means of survival. It was what we did; it was what every islander did. We had morning chores and after-school duties, all of which revolved around housework, food preparation, and taking care of the animals.

Above: *The interior of the First Union African Baptist Church, a place of prayer and worship.* Below: *Daufuskie oysters were a prime source of income for members of Sallie's family and other islanders from the 1920s to the 1940s—and they still make good eating.*

To balance the work, though, we always found time for play. Whenever we could get away from our household and outdoor chores, we loved nothing better than to play in the woods and by the water—creeks, ocean, and sound. Whenever we would come in hungry, Momma and Grandmomma, our aunts and cousins, whoever was cooking, would have a big pot of something on the woodstove. It may have been okra, shrimp, and rice cooked up in a gumbo, or it may have been boiled crabs to go with Momma's preserved okra and tomatoes. Maybe it was just a cake of cornbread; but whatever was cooking, we were thankful for it because we played hard and we worked hard on Daufuskie.

Water

We valued water more when we didn't have to pay for it.

Pumping water from our hand pump that sat under a big tree beyond the backyard was something we did two or three times a day.

A metal pipe was driven into the earth. It had a head-shaped piece with a long mouth and a long handle screwed on to it. All it took to bring forth the water was to pour a small amount of water into the top of the pump and then, with fast hands, pump with one hand and pour water into it with other hand. Up would come the crystal-clear water, fresh and cool from the earth even on hot summer days.

Used for drinking, cooking, and cleaning, it was always the one thing we didn't have to worry about, unless there was a hard freeze, which seldom happened. When we knew a freeze was coming, Momma and Pop would first make us fill every container we could find, including pots and pans. When the pump froze, we had to heat some of the water and pour it into the top of the pump and sometimes around the pipes that go into the ground. This would help melt the ice in the pump pipe and release the water from underneath. At times, Momma and Pop would have to build a small fire around the pipe that went into the ground to help melt the ice and release the water.

The animals that we raised and many other creatures as well would wander near the pump to get a refreshing drink from a big pail that we

A bushel basket of crabs, ready to be picked for one of Sallie's favorite dishes.

Fallen trees on Bloody Point at the southern end of Daufuskie Island.

An ancestral graveyard, nearly washed away by the tides of the Bloody Point River.

left full for them at all times. For fun in the hot summertime, we children would run and jump in and out of a washtub filled with cool water in the backyard.

Washday

Just as each day had its own rhythm—morning chores, school, play, evening chores—so did each week.

We dreaded Saturdays because that is when we did our washing. We would start as early as day clean (which is what we called the part of the morning when the sun wasn't quite over the treetops) and spend all day getting it done. If the weather was warm or hot, we would wash clothes in the backyard. If it was really cold and windy, Momma would set up a wash bench on the back porch with all the tubs. When the heart of winter hit and the northeast wind began blowing stronger and the temperature dropped

*Sallie's grandmother's headstone; in the foreground is a plant native islanders
call "silk grass root," which they once used to make their hair grow.*

low, the clothes would freeze after we hung them out to dry. With all those kids that Momma and Pop shared (they had eight children between them when they started their lives together, and then added two more), mounds of clothes piled up to be washed every single week.

Three or sometimes four tubs, lined up in order, stood next to one another in a row against the corner of the house or on the porch. Another blackened washtub or a barrel of boiling hot water was placed at a distance with a roaring fire under it even in the hot part of the year. It was far away enough for safety, but close enough to help make the job easier; we would use a foot tub bucket for dipping and transporting. Momma believed that the white clothes weren't going to be their whitest unless they were washed, bleached, and scalded in hot water. The hot water was poured in each washtub to the halfway point, then about a third that amount of cold water was added. The rinse water would be even hotter. In between the tubs for washing and rinsing was a foot tub or plastic bucket half filled with beach and water. This was for the light and white clothes that needed bleaching.

Part of the water heating in the tub outside over the open fire was used for Momma's homemade starch. The tub or bucket for clothes that needed to be starched sat at the far end of the wash bench next to the rinse water tub. Most of the pieces to be starched were Momma's Sunday tablecloths, our Sunday dresses, and Pop's good khaki pants that he would wear on Sundays or for an outing on Captain Sam's boat. (Captain Sam ran a ferry out of Savannah.) Momma's homemade starch was good, and she knew how to make it just right for every piece. It was made with plain or self-rising flour and water, slowly mixed, cooked on the woodstove in the house, and stirred constantly to keep it from getting lumpy. One of my sisters or I had the job of cooking the starch exactly the way Momma showed us. Then we would pour it into the large tub of hot water outside, measured in the right amount. Each time the water was lowered from the hot water tub, more had to be pumped to replace it.

Because we were smaller than Momma, she would have a stool for us to climb up on so that we could bend over the washboard to scrub the clothes. Momma would make sure that we washed the clothes clean, or else we had to do it over.

Sallie holding a branch of a chinkapin tree. The tree produces a small nut grown in a sticky outer shell that she and other native kids used to pick and eat in season. They also strung the nuts into necklaces and bracelets that they wore.

*Mullein, also known as deer tongue, is an herb that grows all over Daufuskie;
natives used it to treat sore, swollen muscles.*

I clearly remember rinsing the clothes and hanging them out to dry on the many clotheslines that Momma had strung across the yard, attached to the side of the house. She would watch the sun rise and set the day before washday, and then she would place the lines on the corner of the house so that the sun would hit the clothes as it was coming and going. The clothesline was always out of the way, not in the path to the door or where somebody could stir up a lot of dust and get the clothes dirty again.

After washing loads of clothes all day, not to mention the other jobs we were responsible for, everyone would be ready to sit down and enjoy a good meal.

Sunday was the Lord's Day. We got up just as early as always, did our regular chores, ate breakfast, and went to church. Afterward, extra work was limited. It if wasn't planting season, Pop would do one of his two favorite things: either he would stay home and sit in his favorite chair on the front porch or in a corner in the living room, knitting on his mullet or shrimp nets, or he would go into the river to catch mullet, shrimp, or whatever else was running.

Playtime

Sometimes we found ways to mix work and play. If friends came over while we were working, they would be expected to join in. I was always pleased to finish with the housework so that we could go outside and have all kinds of fun. Our imaginations were wide open; as we kept our spirits high, nothing got in our way. We played many outside games, including Little Sally Walker, ring around the Rosie, big bad Indian, hopscotch, marbles, play house, hide-and-seek, London Bridge, dodgeball, tag, tic-tac-toe (in the sand with sticks), jump rope, limbo rock, freeze tag, baseball, basketball, volleyball, and football, as well as Simon says and other guessing games. We just couldn't get enough of these games. Our friends and family were always ready to be a part of any game we wanted to play.

I can remember when I got my first bike: it was an old, used blue bicycle, but to me, it was like receiving a brand new one. The kids on Daufuskie received lots of other toys that Christmas, when I was about eight years

Sallie shows off spotted mint, which grows wild on Daufuskie, and was used by many natives to make a delicious herbal tea.

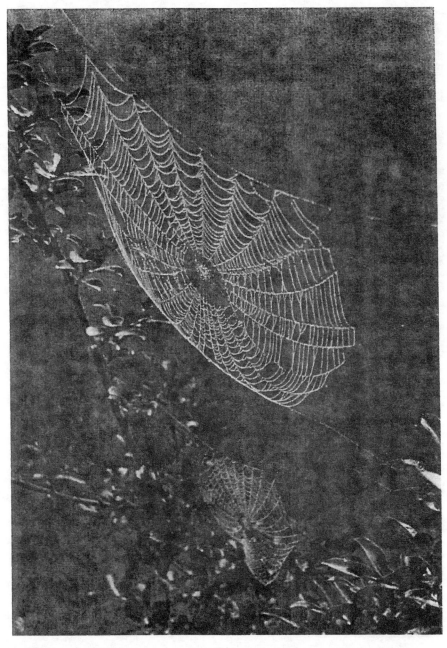

Spiderwebs, such as these growing on an island shrub, were once used by natives to stop the bleeding and seal the wound when they had a scrape or cut.

old, but I fell in love with this bike as if it were the only toy that came, even though I had to share it with my sisters any time they wanted to use it. The worst thing was that I didn't know how to ride a bike; I would have given anything to know how. Every chance I got, I would get on the bike to ride, but I didn't know how to balance myself, so I kept falling off.

Several days later Pop sat on the front porch watching me and shaking his head; I just couldn't keep my balance long enough to ride. He walked over, grabbed the bike by the seat, and said, "I'm gonna show ya on disyah bike and I want ya ta see wayah gwine." Pop held on tight to the back end of my bike seat, I climbed up on the bike, smiling and holding tight. Getting my balance and breathing hard, I said to myself, "I ain't scared. I can ride disyah bike." With this thought and praying hard, plus a good solid push forward from Pop, I was peddling my bike with joy and laughter. I was riding without stopping, and did it ever feel good.

I was so happy, I kept getting up on my bike and riding up and down the road in front of our house. My fear was gone, my balance kept getting better, and I will always remember how much fun it was to learn how to ride a bicycle for the first time.

From sunup to sundown, we worked and played hard, sometimes meeting new challenges, none too hard for us to overcome. Family, neighbors, and friends were a part of our daily living. They brought happiness and togetherness to our community, and no one was different, even though some had more than others. Everyone was loved with respect, whether they were beenyahs or comeyahs."

Changes

If you think change is slow where you are, you should have lived on Daufuskie when I was little. We had no telephones in our homes—there was only one on the island. My family had no electricity until the early 1960s, and even then it was not very reliable and would go out with the slightest wind and during every storm. Pat Conroy's title *The Water Is Wide* really captured the sense of the distance between the mainland and our island in the 1960s. We kids knew nothing about the world beyond our

A castor bean plant growing in a native islander's yard. Though the plant's beans are the source of castor oil, which Sallie and other island children were given by their parents, the beans themselves are poisonous, and island kids were warned not to eat any part of the plant.

little island. But with Mr. Conroy's year on Daufuskie and the publication of his book, change happened more quickly. Vista volunteers came to the island; anthropologists came to study our lives. Most significantly, developers were discovering the beauty of our land.

Parts of Daufuskie today are almost unrecognizable to us: huge houses and gated communities have replaced our islandwide playground. Our imaginary tea parties have been replaced by tee times. Satellite dishes and cell phones are as common as alligators and osprey used to be. Still, when I close my eyes and start to remember, I can smell the pluff mud and hear the seagulls; in my mind I am back in my Gullah girlhood on my Gullah Island.

Then I did not know why we did the things we did; but looking back, I see that we were part of a centuries-old culture of connectedness. We helped each other out with food, with problems, with illnesses. When technology and quick fixes were not around, we had to find our own solutions; we used our minds, not money, to solve problems. And we learned that manners would take us where money would not.

Daufuskie Island existed as a sustainable culture before that became a buzzword of the twenty-first century. We did not worry about what we did not have; we were not in a hurry all the time; we learned through experience with the help of our whole village.

For the descendants of the Lowcountry Gullah people, one of the most positive changes has been a renewed interest in learning about and preserving the Gullah heritage. Every year Hilton Head Island hosts a month-long celebration of Gullah Cultural Heritage with tours, art exhibits, and a festival. In the fall of 2004, the U.S. House of Representatives approved a bill to create a Gullah-Geechee Heritage Corridor to tell the story of that heritage. This came after the announcement in the spring of 2004 by the National Trust for Historic Preservation that it was listing the Gullah-Geechee coast as one of the nation's most endangered historic places. A new production of Pat Conroy's *The Water Is Wide* was filmed and released for television audiences in spring 2006.

I am proud of my Gullah heritage, and I am delighted that as the nation begins to recognize my heritage, I can present this second book. As in my

A beautiful oak tree draped with Spanish moss (which some 'Fuskie natives used to put in their shoes to treat high blood pressure) overlooking Benjie's Point on the riverfront.

first cookbook, I offer memories of my years on Daufuskie Island and I share recipes from my grandmother, my mother, and native islanders who are carrying on our traditions.

I hope you will enjoy reading about my childhood on Daufuskie as much as you enjoy sampling these recipes. But do not let the Morning, Noon, and Night chapter divisions mislead you. Should you wish to serve sizzling grilled shrimp along with your island fried grits with onions for breakfast, to spread fruity fig preserves on homemade cheese biscuits for an afternoon snack with orange peel tea, or to put Carolina chili in the slow cooker and enjoy it at the end of a long day, then that's OK, too.

Morning

Day Clean Breakfast

When the rooster crowed cock-a-doodle-doo and the sun crept over the treetops, bringing the beginning of a brand new day, we would say "day is cleaning." Pop would have been awake for more than an hour thinking of all the chores that we needed to do. He would lie quietly until he thought the time had come for us to get up.

He would wait to hear some kind of noise that would let him know that we were awake and getting out of bed. Knowing this, we would slowly place one foot at a time on the floor, stamping it a few times just to make him believe that we were getting up. Sometimes it felt as if we had just gotten into bed when it was time to get up. Pop didn't believe that we girls needed to spend all morning getting ready; "Dere's too much ta be done," he would say. When he did not hear the right kind of "getting up" noise coming from the room, he would yell through the thin walls that connected our bedroom to his and Momma's, saying "Off and on it, cause nuttin' gets done when ya lyin' in bed." After being told this many times, one day I asked him what "off and on it" meant. Looking at me with a half smile, his response was, "Get off ya backside and on ya feet."

Momma would be in the kitchen long before us, rattling pots and pans. The aroma of hot, stiff grits and smothered shrimp with bacon, onions, and green bell pepper, not to mention the smell of homemade biscuits, would scent the whole house.

On winter mornings when the northeast wind was blowing, making it feel much colder outside, Momma would have a roaring fire in the wood heater in the living room warming up the rest of the house. My sisters and I would push each other out of the way to get the best spot to finish dressing near the wood heater. Momma would yell out to us as we got a little play in, "Ya'll churn stop that darn playing." She would remind us that Pop was going to have our hides if we didn't hurry up and get the housework done and the outside animals fed before school at 8 o'clock.

Our days were planned with many chores, whether we liked it or not. We had to refill the wood box behind the woodstove in the kitchen and the wood box behind the heater, and we would pump enough buckets of water to get Momma through the day until we returned. We fed the chickens, slopped the hogs, fed the cats and dogs, and moved the cows to a fresh grassy spot to graze for the rest of the day. All this and more was usually done in record time as we pitched in to help one another.

The morning was not complete until everyone had finished what he or she was doing. Pop would come out of the room to see if we were getting things done. When we had finished all the morning chores, we would gather at the breakfast table to break bread, eating a hearty breakfast that would stick to our ribs until the next meal.

When we were out of the house, Momma always had her hands full with cooking, cleaning, and making sure everything we needed was in place. Momma would get dinner started right after everyone had breakfast and one of us had washed the dishes. She would grumble to herself sometimes, "Women's work is nevah done; the minute you get shrew with one ting, dere's sumptin else waitin'. The housework is nevah done."

Choosing and laying out our school clothes was done nightly. Momma said it kept us from fumbling for something to wear the following morning. She would also have us pick out our Sunday clothes and lay them aside neatly before we went to bed on Saturday night.

Southern Skillet Fried Bread

Sometimes the simplest things made a big difference. Pop had several handicaps, but he made everything seem easy. Pop was crippled in one leg; he said this had happened when he was a small child. Pop was also blind in one eye and always wore dark "sun shades," but we noticed how he never let anything stop or limit him. He would challenge anything small or large and would not be defeated. He helped build my courage with his words of strength: "No matter whacha wanna be, if ya be a ditch diggah, den be da best." Pop always reminded us that the reason he was being hard on us was because of his high hopes for our futures. We didn't know all of his reasons, but I felt he pushed us because he didn't want us to miss out on a good education. Momma and Pop passed their struggles on to us to make us better.

Momma and Pop didn't need any lessons in cooking. They were very good cooks, and we enjoyed every meal. Pop loved to eat bread with most meals, but he said this dish—fried bread without meat—was a poor man's meal. He called this recipe "bread and water," with the understanding that we never forgot the meals that brought us through the hard times. Pop used every opportunity to teach us some wise lessons; he even had a saying about bread: "Half a loaf is betta dan none."

When mixing this batter, the thicker the better.

⅓ cup oil
1½ cups self-rising flour
⅓–½ cup water (you can use milk if you like)

Heat half or less of the oil in a skillet. In a bowl, mix the flour and water together well. Pour one-quarter to one-half of the mixture into the heated skillet and let it fry until it is golden brown on one side. If you are not sure when to flip the batter, wait until little bubbles appear on top as it cooks. Use a spatula to lift the bread and look underneath to see if it is brown enough. Then turn it over and let it cook thoroughly on the other side; remove and place on a plate. Continue to pour the bread batter into the skillet, adding more of the oil as needed, to cook as you did the first time. Once you have cooked all the batter, spread some butter or margarine on the bread, then pour on your favorite syrup. Remember, however you get it, a stomachful is a stomachful.

Crispy Smoked Bacon and Cheese Grits

As the first meal of the day, breakfast is important to get you started on your way. Try cooking bacon in the oven or microwave if you don't like cooking it in a skillet because of the popping grease.

6 slices smoked bacon
1 cup uncooked grits
2 cups water

1 teaspoon salt

4–5 slices American cheese (or other cheese of your choice)

Lay the bacon slices side by side in a baking pan. Place the pan in the oven at 350° and let the bacon cook until it reaches the crispiness you desire. While the bacon is cooking, wash the raw grits twice (yes, wash your grits); put the grits, water, and salt in a medium pot. Stir, place the pot on the stove, and continue to stir regularly, over medium heat, until the grits are done. Good southern grits can be cooked anywhere from 45 minutes to an hour or longer; for me, the longer the better. Grits should not be gritty or crunchy when cooked.

When the grits are almost done, add the cheese slices and stir in well as they melt. Turn the heat down to low until you are ready to serve the grits. When the bacon has completed cooking, drain the grease, and let the slices cool for a few minutes; place them on the side of the plate with the cheese grits and enjoy.

Scrambled Eggs with Onion, Bell Pepper, and Cheese

Preparing your eggs this way is also great for a sandwich.

¼ cup oil

½ small onion, thinly sliced

¼ medium-sized red or green bell pepper, diced

4 large eggs, beaten lightly

¼ cup grated cheddar or American cheese

In a skillet, heat the oil over medium heat; do not overheat. Add the onion and bell pepper; cook, stirring occasionally, for about a minute. Add the eggs; then stir in the cheese and cook until the eggs are as firm as you like. Enjoy your nutritious, quick, and easy breakfast.

Sallie's Best Milk and Egg Toast

Momma would almost always have some kind of milk, whether it be fresh from one of our cows, canned, or powdered. Sometimes she would buy Carnation evaporated milk, which we would dilute, half and half, with water.

The cow gave milk for only about three weeks after having a calf or up to a month if the momma cow was younger. The calf would get his share, and we would get as much as we could. Milking the cow had to be done early in the morning, hopefully before the calf got his. Pop would tell us that the cow breast had dried up when there was not enough to fill a bucket.

To some people we were poor; to others we were better off than most. But we just did what we had to do, and we always did our best. Some island folks lived on a fixed income. Most of what they had was what they grew in their gardens, animals that they raised for meat, wildlife native to the island, and seafood from the water that surrounded the island. Once a month some folks from the mainland would bring cases of government-provided food to the island to help meet our needs. These were supplemental foods like powdered milk and eggs, large chunks of cheese (this made the best macaroni and cheese), and canned pork, turkey, and beef. All of this, with what we worked hard to have, kept food on our table daily.

Over on the mainland others called this dish what they wanted, but to me it was our own discovery. Some mornings I would rush to gather fresh chicken eggs to make my favorite milk and egg toast.

When you are lost for what to fix for breakfast, how about trying this yummy toast? Your family will be pleased that you went the extra mile. Put on your best tablecloth and make it extra special. Give it what you've got with some extra trimming. Make breakfast fun again, even if the milk does not come from your own cow or the eggs do not come straight from your henhouse.

¼ cup oil
4–6 large eggs
1½ cups whole milk

1–2 teaspoons ground cinnamon
1 teaspoon vanilla extract
¼ loaf white or wheat bread
1 cup syrup of your choice

Put the oil in a skillet and heat on medium-high; do not heat the oil to smoking. Meanwhile, in a medium bowl, beat the eggs until they start to fluff. Slowly add the milk to the eggs and mix; then add the cinnamon and vanilla extract. Mix together well. Dip one slice of bread at a time in the milk and egg mixture, coating both sides. Place the soaked bread in the skillet and cook on each side until brown. When the toast is cooked, place it on a plate on top of a paper towel to absorb the excess oil if you like. Serve warm, with plenty of syrup. You and your family or neighbors can enjoy a nice breakfast at home without the expense of going out.

Down-Home Fruity Pancakes

When all else fails, a few tasty pancakes with fruit feed the beenyah soul.

½ cup oil
1½ cups all-purpose flour
1 teaspoon sugar
1 teaspoon baking powder
1–2 large eggs, beaten
1 cup milk or water (you can substitute fruit juice
    for some or all of the liquid)
½–1 cup fruit of your choice

Add half the oil to a skillet and let it heat but not until it is smoking or burning. In a medium-sized mixing bowl, combine the flour, sugar, baking powder, eggs, and milk (or water or fruit juice). Mix these ingredients together well, then add pieces or thin slices of fruit; the batter should be medium-thick. Depending on the size you want your pancakes, spoon medium or large spoonfuls of batter into the heated oil; cook until golden brown, then flip over and let brown on the other side. Repeat, adding more oil as needed, until all the batter is used. Serve these up with butter, syrup, or however your family enjoys them.

TIP: A good time to flip pancakes is when you see little bubbles forming on top of the batter as it cooks.

Island Fried Grits with Onions

I grew up eating lots of grits—served soft, thick, chunky, gravied down, and even with a splash of hot bacon grease when there was no butter. Momma said she fed us grits from the time we were born. In our house grits were the king of the kitchen, and they were one thing Momma and Pop never let run out. We ate grits with meals at any time of the day. And having them for breakfast was a must most mornings. Pop often liked to eat grits at suppertime with his smothered, fresh-caught mullet and sometimes with a hot baked or boiled sweet potato on the side. You talk about some real good eating.

When a big pot of grits was cooked and we didn't eat it all during a meal, the pot was pushed to the back of the woodstove and reused later. It would become one of Pop's favorites: stiff grits.

We were not allowed to throw grits away unless we were feeding them to the animals outside. This happened only when we had little or no regular animal food. Momma and Pop would sometimes have us cook a bigger pot of grits to share among the hogs, dog, and cats.

Our animals were always fed twice a day. If the chickens were turned out of their coop while the cats and dogs were eating their meals, the chickens would take chances to get some of their food. Momma would have us shoo them away so they would not steal the other animals' food. She said she didn't want the laying hens to eat the cooked grits because it would make the shell of the eggs soft when the hens lay.

The taste of leftover grits was just as good. Momma had a favorite way of eating her grits right out of the pot with lots of milk and some butter. I liked that myself.

Wasting food in our house was called being "long eyed"—when you wanted more than your stomach could hold. The next time you have some leftover grits, you just might want to try this recipe.

2–3 teaspoons butter or oil
1 small onion, sliced (thin or thick, as you prefer)
1–2 cups cold or room-temperature cooked grits

Heat the butter or oil in a medium-sized skillet. When using butter, don't turn the heat up too high. Add the onion slices and let them cook until they are clear. Add the grits and let them fry, stirring them to break them down. When the grits are heated through, serve them on a plate and add whatever you like to go with them.

Country Fried Fish with Grits

Especially when the fish were biting, we ate a lot of fish and grits. We would add a little splash of grease if there was no butter or gravy. The different varieties of fish we caught and ate were mullet, whiting, flounder, catfish, croaker, trout, yellow tail, spots, and sometimes bass and sheephead, which were the hardest to catch. All are very tasty and can be fried, smothered, grilled, broiled, baked, and even barbecued. Momma also loved to eat that wiggly fish called an eel. She knew that she was the only one who would eat it, so she got to eat it all by herself. The rest of us would never put an eel in our mouths because it looked too much like a snake.

Eating a lot of fish is good for you. We never got enough of catching and eating the different kinds that could be found in the waterways of Daufuskie. We used to be able to sit on any riverbank or dock and catch a meal or enough to share with others any time of the day or night. I remember times when Pop would return from the mullet hole with bushel baskets and croaker sacks full of mullets still jumping. Momma's face would light up as she would have us girls get a knife and pitch in for the scraping and cleaning. Momma would later wash, season, and fry up a big pan of mullet, bake a large pan of sweet cornbread, and have us wash and grease some sweet potatoes to put in the woodstove to bake.

When the meal was ready, so were we. We would all gather around the table to eat. Pop used to say, "Elbow buckle and mouth fly open." If you think about it, this is what happens when you are eating. Before long our mouths and hands would be greasy, and our bellies would be full. We would clean the dishes and ourselves and go to bed looking forward to the next day.

The next morning Momma would add some onion and water to any leftover fried fish, and we would eat them on some more grits, stiff or not.

Frying fish is easy; the key is seasoning it to your own taste.

1½–2 cups oil
6 medium-sized fish, scaled and cleaned
sprinkle salt and black pepper on both sides
sprinkle paprika on both sides
sprinkle garlic powder on both sides (optional)
1–2 cups flour

Place the oil in a skillet and heat at medium-high. Wash the fish and pat dry; season with salt, pepper, paprika, and garlic powder. Put the flour in a paper bag or a bowl and place one or two fish at a time in flour; shake or stir the fish to coat well with flour, and then shake excess flour off before adding the fish to the heated oil. Let fry to your desired texture, soft or hard. Remove from the oil and let cool a bit before serving. Hot fish is good, but a burned tongue is painful.

Preserving It

As the seasons changed from bitter cold to warm and sunny, the fruits, berries, nuts, and vegetables ripened. My younger sisters and I loved this time of year even though we knew that we had our work cut out for us.

Momma would have us gather the bounty by the foot tubs or bushel baskets to be peeled and cut. My sisters and I would fill up on the fruits and vegetables, eating them throughout the day. Momma had to warn us constantly not to eat more than we cut. My sister and I would smile at each other, hoping Momma wasn't looking while we snuck another piece of fruit into our mouths.

Days before the peeling and cutting, we would collect the jars and their lids so that Momma could sterilize them for the preserves. Momma had several large canning pots set aside especially for cooking and sealing her preserves. No one was allowed to use them for anything else. She would say the pot needed to stay fresh just for her preserving. If you cooked some other food in the preserving pots, the scent of the food could get into the special preserves.

Bushel baskets and foot tubs full of pears, peaches, figs, and apples had to be picked, cleaned, peeled, cored, and cut. The baskets and tubs full of squash, tomatoes, beans, peas, and okra (which I didn't get too close to) had to be cut up or shelled. My sisters and I would shake our heads at all the work. Never mind how we felt, we knew better than to let Momma or Pop see the anger on our faces.

Momma would spend hours in the hot kitchen getting things together while we were outside on the front porch, catching a cool breeze as we peeled, shelled, and cut. Sometimes Pop would have us do the work at the dining room table so he could keep an eye on us. He would be sitting in his favorite chair across from us knitting on his nets. He would tell us jokes and stories about times when he was growing up and the people who once lived on the island. Sometimes the stories would be so funny Momma would get mad at Pop, thinking he wasn't letting us get our work done. Pop was a great storyteller, and he knew that his stories would help us keep our interest in what we were doing.

It seemed to take days of peeling, shelling, and cutting the fruits and vegetables, combined with our other work around the house, but we knew that our reward would be a taste of Momma's good homemade preserves. Momma would let us take turns helping her in the kitchen; she always felt that it was necessary to show us the way she did things, just the way her momma showed her. Being the oldest, I would get the most time in the kitchen with her because she needed me to take care of things when she and Pop were gone from the house. Of course, they left only to go over to the mainland, or to fish, crab, or pick gallons of oysters.

When the job was all done and the jars were stacked neatly on the shelf or in a safe corner, Momma would be proud to look at all her jars full of preserved fruits and vegetables. Her face would light up as she counted them one by one. She would then cover them with a white tablecloth or an old sheet. Momma knew that all this hard work would be on our dinner table come the cold winter months.

Momma and Pop would explain the importance of preserving summer's bounty for later. Pop made certain he reminded us of the cold winter days and nights when the northeast wind would start blowing outside, and we would have to stay inside; having preserved the foods we liked helped make those days better so that we would be able to eat a bellyful. Good times or bad times, cold, rain, sleet, or wind, these preserved fruits and vegetables were always good on the table for breakfast, lunch, and dinner. Momma would often share her great preserves with folks from the mainland.

Today, I love what I do, sharing these recipes that Momma used to keep close to her apron. Now do it just the way I tell you.

Notes on Preserving

For those of you who want to try these recipes but haven't canned anything before, here are a few tips that may help you.

1. In the canning pot used for sterilizing the lids and the jars before they are filled, place enough water to cover the jars completely as it boils.

2. Fill hot jars almost to the top with preserves. Wipe the rim of the jar with a cloth to be sure it is clean.

3. Place lids on the hot jars containing preserves and loosely tighten. Do not tighten the lids completely.

4. After the jars are filled and the lids are on, you are ready to complete the process of sealing. You may use the same canning pot you used for sterilizing or a different, sterilized pot. Begin with 3 to 4 inches of water. Let it come to a boil, and then add the jars with fruit or vegetables. Add more hot water to cover the jars. Boil for the time recommended in each recipe.

5. For safety reasons, do not let the jars touch each other.

6. After processing the jars of preserves in the water bath for the time indicated, remove them from the water and let them cool.

Jammin' Grape Jelly

In the spring on Daufuskie, the birds and the animals get ready to mate again and have their young ones, and the bare trees and branches all turn green. My sisters and I could hardly wait to take off our many layers of clothes and our shoes and run around with bare feet in the smooth, gritty sand. Momma would have us open all the shutters and raise the windows throughout the house so that the fresh spring air could blow through. We would begin to see more and more birds; bees, butterflies, grasshoppers, and other bugs would start to show up everywhere.

Spring comes in strong on the island, and the fruit trees and berry bushes fill up fast with new leaves day by day. When the blossoms on the trees began to open, my sisters and I would try to count them. We would watch the changes on the trees as the blossoms became little fruits or berries. We wished our gardens could grow that way on their own; we wanted less work and more play.

Time passed quickly, and the fruits and berries grew bigger as they ripened. The birds would always try to get their share before the fruits and berries were ripe. We knew we had our work cut out for us as we began to gather the ripe fruits and berries early each day so that the birds and animals would not beat us to them.

The grapevines were draped with bunches of sweet, juicy grapes getting bigger every day. If it happened to rain while the grapes were growing, Momma would have a big smile on her face, because she knew that would make the grapes bigger and sweeter. Many grapevines grew in our backyard and along the roadside on Daufuskie. These grapes grew out in the wild on their own. The wild grapes were just one of many of nature's fruits that were plentiful for anyone to enjoy. The roadside belonged to everyone.

8–10 cups black grapes

6–7 cups granulated sugar, divided

1 tablespoon lemon juice

Wash the grapes and remove all stems while the canning jars and lids are being sterilized in a large pot of boiling water. Place the whole grapes in a large pot with half the sugar and the lemon juice; let them cook on medium-high until the grape skins break open, no more than 15 to 20 minutes. Do not add water. Strain the grapes through cheesecloth or a fine mesh strainer into another pot. For every 1 cup of juice, add ⅔ cup sugar. Boil for about 25 to 30 minutes, stirring frequently. The mixture will be ready when the juice drips thickly from the spoon. Follow the steps for processing in the Notes on Preserving (page 00), boiling for 10 to 15 minutes.

Sassy Strawberry Preserves

4 pints fresh strawberries
6–8 cups sugar
2–2½ cups water

Hull and wash the strawberries and place them in a medium to large pot; add the sugar and water; let come to a slow boil at medium heat. Stir occasionally until the mixture thickens. As it thickens, stir more frequently to prevent scorching. When the strawberries have cooked down and thickened, ready for jarring, remove the pot from the heat and let it sit for a short while. Follow the steps for processing in the Notes on Preserving (page 00), boiling for 10 to 15 minutes.

Precious Pear Preserves

15–20 medium pears, peeled, cored, and cut into wedges
4–6 cups sugar
½ teaspoon ground allspice
1 teaspoon ground nutmeg

1 teaspoon ground cinnamon
6–8 whole cloves
grated zest of ½ lemon
½–1 cup water

Place the pear wedges in a medium-sized pot over medium heat. Add the sugar, allspice, nutmeg, cinnamon, cloves, lemon zest, and water. Let simmer; the pears will turn reddish as they cook; the mixture will cook down. Follow the steps for processing in the Notes on Preserving (page 00), boiling for 10 to 15 minutes.

Fruity Fig Preserves

6 pounds fresh figs
6 cups sugar
1 quart water
1½ teaspoons ground cinnamon
1 teaspoon ground cloves
juice of 1 lemon

Put the sugar and water in a pot and bring to a boil; cook until the sugar dissolves. Wash the figs gently and add them to the pot. Then add the cinnamon, cloves, and lemon juice. Let boil on medium heat for about 25 minutes, or until the figs are tender and translucent. Remove the figs from the syrup with a slotted spoon. Let the syrup boil for 10 more minutes, or until it reaches the consistency you desire. Return the figs to the syrup; remove from heat; skim off any foam with a spoon. Follow the steps for processing in the Notes on Preserving (page 00), boiling for 8 to 10 minutes.

Willing Watermelon Rind Preserves

I can't tell you how many times my sisters, cousins, and other island children would sit in our grandparents' watermelon field eating until we couldn't move. We would burst the melon open right in the field because we were not allowed to bring a knife outside.

Grandmomma had a hand for growing watermelons, along with the other fruits and vegetables that she loved to eat. Near the end of the season she would send us into her watermelon patch to pick all that she wanted. We would pick dozens and line most of them up on the front porch, putting a few under the kitchen table as well. She would share her melons with islanders who could not get out to plant for themselves. Then she would turn us loose in the field to eat as much as we wanted.

Grandmomma used to plant several varieties of melons, which grew to be different sizes. Sometimes they would rot or split open from too much sun and not enough rain during their growing season. These she would give to the hogs as a snack; we loved to throw the watermelons into the hog pen, bursting them wide open. It was fun to watch the hogs gobble them up.

There is an old saying about planting: a garden will grow best for two types of people when they drop the seeds: a pregnant woman and a small child. Both are growing, one is growing upward as the other is growing outward. That was one reason Pop and Momma would have us kids drop most of the seeds when it came to planting time. Pop would say, "Jus' like ya churn springin' up, so do dem seeds in da dirt."

3 quarts watermelon rind, cut into pieces ¼ inch or smaller
3–4 tablespoons salt
6 quarts water, divided
6–8 cups granulated sugar (or brown sugar, if you prefer)
½ cup lemon juice
grated zest of ½ lemon
1 heaping tablespoon ground ginger

Wipe the watermelon all over with a damp cloth to remove any dirt before cutting. Working on a sturdy surface, cut the watermelon in half lengthwise. Use a large spoon or scoop to remove most of the watermelon. Leave about ¼ inch or less of the red inside the rind. Slice the rind into strips, then into pieces about ¼ inch or smaller.

Dissolve the salt in 4 quarts of warm water, and pour it over the melon rind in a large bowl or pot. Let sit for at least 30 minutes. Drain and rinse the rind in cool water. Drain again and place the rind in a medium or large pot. Sprinkle the sugar, lemon juice and zest, and ginger over the rind, add 2 quarts of warm water, and place the pot on the stove on medium heat. Let cook, stirring occasionally to prevent sticking.

Cook until the watermelon rind is tender and clear, 20 to 30 minutes. Let cool. Handle with care, because the hot, sticky syrup can cause a bad burn. Mash the rind with a potato masher or fork to make the preserves spreadable. Follow the steps for processing in the Notes on Preserving (page 00), boiling for 10 to 15 minutes.

Prissy Peach Preserves

~~~~~~

10 cups peeled, pitted, sliced peaches
3 cups sugar
1 tablespoon water
2–3 teaspoons lemon juice

Wash the peaches before peeling and cutting them. Place them in a medium to large pot; add the sugar, water, and lemon juice. Cook on medium heat, bringing to a slow boil. Watch closely and stir occasionally as the sugar dissolves and the sauce thickens. Let the preserves cook for about 25 to 35 minutes. Remove from heat and scoop off any foam. Follow the steps for processing in the Notes on Preserving (page 00), boiling for 10 to 15 minutes.

Blackberry Preserves

4 quarts ripe blackberries
⅓ cup water
8 cups sugar

Wash the berries carefully in a colander under running water. Place the berries in a medium to large pot along with the water and sugar. Let cook on medium heat until the mixture starts to boil; turn the heat down and stir occasionally until the preserves thicken. Follow the steps for processing in the Notes on Preserving (page oo), boiling for 10 to 15 minutes.

Momma's Preserved Okra and Tomatoes

For many native islanders, okra and tomatoes go together. Sometimes Momma would jar them separately as well as together. Momma made sure when she was ready to cook she had her choice. I remember the years when Grandmomma's okra field was full of beautiful yellow blossoms ready to become pods of okra; after every cutting, more and more would grow. At home Momma and Pop did not grow as much okra, but they grew more tomatoes. The plants would hang with so many tomatoes they touched the ground. Momma would show us how to put sticks under the limbs to prop them up. Momma would have my sisters and me haul a basket of tomatoes to Grandmomma's and bring back a basketful of okra in exchange. Of course, I wouldn't get near the okra. I just couldn't stand the smell of okra; it drove me away.

12–15 pounds ripe but firm tomatoes
6 pounds okra, cut up
1 large onion, diced
2 tablespoons bacon grease
2 quarts hot water

1 tablespoon sugar or less
4½ teaspoons salt

Unless you prefer to leave the skins on the tomatoes, bring a medium pot of water for blanching to boil on the stove. Wash the tomatoes and remove any stems before placing them in the hot water; when the skin starts to peel off easily, remove from the hot water. Use a scoop or long-handled spoon to protect yourself as you add and remove tomatoes from hot water After the tomatoes cool enough to remove the skins completely, cut them into quarters or smaller pieces.

In another pot, heat the bacon grease and add the okra and onion; let cook for about 2 to 3 minutes. Combine the okra and onion with the tomatoes, water, sugar, and salt; stir and taste, and adjust the sugar or salt if necessary, then let simmer. Let cook for about 10 to 15 minutes. Follow the steps for processing in the Notes on Preserving (page 00), boiling for 20 to 30 minutes.

Preserved String Beans and Tadas

3–6 strips fatback bacon
10 pounds string beans
1 large onion, diced
6 cups water
salt and black pepper to taste
3–5 pounds white or red potatoes, peeled and
    cut into ¼- to ½-inch pieces

In a large pot, fry the fatback bacon. Break the tips off both ends of the string beans and snap the beans in half. Add the beans, onion, water, salt, and pepper to the bacon and grease in the pot. Let come to a slow boil and cook until the beans start to get tender. Add the potatoes and let cook until tender (until you can stick a fork into them without force). Let the cooked vegetables cool enough to put in sterile jars and follow the steps for processing in the Notes on Preserving (page 00), boiling for 20 to 30 minutes.

Muffins

Momma didn't have any recipes saved in a box to remind her how to make things; all she had was what was in her head and her taste buds to let her know that her dishes were good. She made many meals by being creative with what she had. If she didn't have something, she didn't worry about it or let it stop her from making a great meal or dessert. We never knew how she made so many tasty meals with so little.

Like Momma, many of the island ladies had a way with their tasty meals. Some kind of meal was always cooked and the native islanders were ready to welcome anyone to their tables. It was all about being a good neighbor and being country folks.

Cornbread, muffins, cakes, pies, and cobblers are all great desserts, and the ladies on Daufuskie knew how to fix really good ones. We enjoyed eating many desserts made with fresh-picked fruits and berries during their season. Not having a store around the corner in the off-season where we could get frozen fruits and berries did not bother us. We never missed what we didn't have. These muffins—whether served for breakfast or for dessert—are a few of the kinds that Momma would bake for us.

TIP: Because ovens do not all heat or hold heat the same, it is usually a good idea to do the toothpick test on muffins. Insert a toothpick in the center of the muffin and then pull it out; if it comes out clean, the muffin is done.

Carolina Blueberry Muffins

Makes 2 dozen.

2½ cups all-purpose flour
⅔ cup sugar
1 tablespoon baking soda
½ teaspoon salt
4 large eggs, beaten

8 tablespoons melted butter
1½ cups milk
2 teaspoons vanilla extract
1½ to 2 cups fresh or frozen blueberries

Preheat oven to 375°. In a medium bowl, combine the flour, sugar, baking soda, and salt. Add the eggs, butter, milk, and vanilla extract, combining well. Gently fold in the washed and drained blueberries. Whether you use a greased muffin pan or paper cup liners, spoon the batter into the cups so that they are about two-thirds full. Bake for 20 to 30 minutes or until golden brown. Let cool and enjoy.

Homemade Apple Nut Cinnamon Muffins

Makes 1 dozen.

2 cups all-purpose flour
½ cup sugar
1 tablespoon baking powder
½ teaspoon cinnamon
½ teaspoon salt
½ cup butter or margarine
1½ cups peeled and diced apples
⅔ cup chopped walnuts
1 large egg
⅔ cup milk

Topping
1½ teaspoons cinnamon
1½ tablespoons brown sugar

Preheat oven to 400°. If you peel and dice the apples ahead of time, place them in lemon juice to keep them from turning brown, then drain them when it's time to add them to the muffin batter. In a bowl, sift together the flour, sugar, baking powder, cinnamon, and salt. Using a knife, cut in the butter. Add the apples and walnuts to the flour mixture. In a separate bowl, beat the egg and milk together; then add them to the flour mixture. Stir only until blended (the batter should be a little lumpy). Spoon the batter into greased muffin pan cups or paper liners, about two-thirds full. For the topping, combine the cinnamon and brown sugar and sprinkle over the batter in the muffin pan. Bake for 15 to 20 minutes.

Comeyah Banana Nut Muffins

Makes 2½ dozen.

4 cups all-purpose flour
2 teaspoons baking soda
2 teaspoons baking powder
½ teaspoon salt
1 teaspoon ground cinnamon
½ teaspoon ground nutmeg or grated fresh nutmeg
1 cup walnuts, chopped
2 large eggs
⅔ cup sugar
⅔ cup milk
½ cup vegetable oil
5–6 large ripe bananas

Preheat oven to 375°. In a mixing bowl, sift together the flour, baking soda, baking powder, salt, cinnamon, and nutmeg; add the nuts to this mixture. In a second bowl, combine the eggs, sugar, milk, and oil. In a third bowl, beat the bananas with a mixer or mash them with a fork. Mix the bananas into the liquid ingredients. Combine the dry and wet mixtures, at low speed if you are using a mixer. Whether you use paper liners or greased muffin pans, fill each muffin cup about two-thirds full. Bake for about 25 to 30 minutes. You'll love 'em.

Grandmomma's Sweet Tada Muffins

Makes about 2 dozen.

1½ cups self-rising flour
⅓ cup sugar
½ teaspoon ground cinnamon
1 teaspoon ground nutmeg
½ cup vegetable oil
½ cup pure maple syrup
2 large eggs, beaten
1 teaspoon vanilla extract
1½ cups mashed cooked sweet potatoes
½ cup raisins and/or walnuts

Grease muffin pans or use paper liners. Preheat oven to about 350° to 375°. In a bowl, sift together the flour, sugar, cinnamon, and nutmeg. In a separate bowl, combine the oil, maple syrup, eggs, and vanilla extract. Stir the sweet potatoes, raisins, and/or nuts into the oil mixture and add the wet mixture to the dry ingredients. Blend together well; fill muffin cups about two-thirds full. Bake for 25 to 30 minutes.

Gullah Bacon Corn Muffins

Makes about 2½ dozen.

14–16 slices crisp bacon (fried, microwaved, or oven baked,
    drained on a paper towel to remove excess grease)
4–6 teaspoons margarine or butter
2 cups all-purpose flour
2 tablespoons baking powder
1½ teaspoons sugar
3 cups cornmeal

1 teaspoon salt
2½ cups milk
3 large eggs

Preheat oven to 350°. Chop the bacon into small pieces and set aside. Melt the margarine or butter and set aside. Sift together the flour, baking powder, sugar, cornmeal, and salt in a large bowl. In a saucepan, heat the milk to lukewarm. In a medium bowl, beat the eggs, then blend in the warm milk and melted margarine or butter. Combine with the flour mixture; fold in bacon pieces mixing all together. Spoon mixture in paper liners or greased muffin pan cups until about half full. Bake until done—about 25 minutes. Serve hot or warm for best taste.

Hearty Oatmeal Raisin Muffins

Makes 1 dozen.

When I make this recipe, I think of my granddaddy from Daufuskie; he was a small man with a hearty appetite. Granddaddy liked to tell us stories about working for a dollar a day on a dredge called the *Cleveland* or about how, when he was a child, he could nearly walk from Daufuskie Island to Hilton Head Island at low tide.

For years he loved to start his mornings with a big, hot bowl of oatmeal. It helped keep him strong, healthy, and wise. Granddaddy Joseph lived to be 96 years old, and he never complained about anything. Most people who knew him said he was a peaceful and quiet man.

1 cup oats
1 cup milk
1 stick butter or margarine at room temperature
½ cup dark brown sugar, firmly packed
1 large egg, beaten
1 cup all-purpose flour
1 teaspoon baking powder

½ teaspoon baking soda
¼ teaspoon salt
⅔ cup raisins

In a medium bowl, combine the oats and milk and let soak for 30 minutes. While you are waiting for the oats to soften, preheat the oven to 400° and grease muffin pans if you are not using paper liners. Use an electric mixer to cream the butter and brown sugar until light and fluffy. Mix in the egg. In another bowl, sift together the flour, baking powder, baking soda, and salt; add the raisins to this mixture. Combine the moist and dry ingredients and add the oat and milk mixture. Do not overmix. Spoon the muffin cups two-thirds full of batter and bake for 20 to 25 minutes, or until done.

Momma's Crackling Muffins

Makes about 1 dozen.

Crackling was a good part of our diet. When it was hog killing time, Momma could hardly wait to gather the fat that lined the belly of the hog. She would have Pop put some of the hog skin in a large pan with the fat. She would then call us girls to the kitchen to help her, and she would teach us how to make crackling.

She scolded us not to get any sand on the fat or it would not be any good. Getting sand on the fat is like getting sand in glue. You can't wash the sand off the fat; it has to be cut off and thrown away. Momma didn't want to waste any of her fat that way.

She would show us how to cut the fat and place it in a large pot for frying on medium heat. Cooking on heat that was too high was not good. Watching carefully so the fat cooked the right way was important for crackling. We had to stand next to the woodstove and watch the fat as it fried down, making sure that it did not cook too fast and burn. When the pork skin was cooked, the skin with some fat on it would become very crunchy and crackly, thus the name "crackling."

We had to be careful in handling hot grease. It could cause a very bad burn.

When the fat and skin had completely cooked and then cooled a little, Momma would pour the hog fat liquid into a container that would not melt or break. When the hog fat cooled down completely, it became lard, which was used for many of Momma's cooking needs. Momma would stack several containers of lard on a shelf in a corner or in the cupboard.

When we were out of hair grease, Pop used to tell us to use some lard in our hair. He said we would only smell like food walking around. We knew he had to be joking because that was not funny. We were pretty sure we didn't want our hair to smell like the food we ate.

Crackling is tasty if you like to chew on something hard and crunchy. It made a good snack for us in the country. Momma loved making her crackling muffins; they were great muffins with a crunchy chew in every bite.

1 cup cornmeal
½ cup all-purpose flour
¼ cup sugar
2 teaspoons baking powder
½ teaspoon salt
¾ cup milk or buttermilk
2 large eggs, beaten
⅔ cup crackling
½ cup melted shortening

In a bowl, combine the cornmeal, flour, sugar, baking powder, and salt. Mix in the milk and eggs. Gradually stir in the crackling and shortening. If the crackling pieces are too big, break them down. Grease a muffin pan or use paper liners; fill each cup two-thirds full, leaving room for the batter to rise. Bake at 375° for about 30 to 35 minutes.

Noon

Sandwiches

Being a southern country girl, born and raised on an island without a bridge in a place that some folks would call the sticks, I can say that I've been blessed to know hard times. I learned what they were like growing up on Daufuskie. Each day was a challenge for us as kids. But poor or not, we ate like kings and queens, and we shared with those that needed our help. Hard work and good food went together; it was as if we had to do one in order to get and enjoy the other. Our gathering together at the table was a special time for us. While people in many places were moving away from the old-fashioned ways, we stayed the same.

Cooking is a passion for me, and I love to share what I cook because it is also a gift and an art. Food tastes like what you put into it. As long as you add some love to your "fixin' and mixin'," then love is going to be what you get back.

These are some of my favorite sandwiches, and I hope you enjoy them as much as I do.

Fried Shrimp Sandwich with Lettuce and Tomato

Makes 2 or 3 sandwiches. Wow! What a great sandwich to fix and eat.

1 dozen large or jumbo shrimp, peeled, deveined, and split open
1 teaspoon salt
1 teaspoon black pepper
1 heaping teaspoon garlic powder
1 teaspoon paprika
1½ cups oil
1 medium-sized onion, sliced in rings
1 large egg
½ cup milk (whole or skim)
1 cup flour

For Each Sandwich
1 teaspoon mayonnaise
1 teaspoon mustard
2 slices bread
1–2 pieces lettuce
1–2 slices tomato

Wash and drain the shrimp; use a paper towel to remove excess water if necessary. Place the shrimp in a medium bowl and add the salt, pepper, garlic powder, and paprika. Toss the shrimp to coat with the seasoning and then set aside in the refrigerator until ready to use.

Heat the oil in a skillet over medium heat. When it gets hot, add the onion slices and sauté. When the onion is as soft as you like it, remove it from the oil. Leave the oil in the skillet with the heat on very low until you are ready to fry the shrimp.

Beat the egg and milk together well in a bowl. Put the flour in another bowl or in a paper or plastic bag. Turn heat under the oil to medium-high for frying. Remove the seasoned shrimp from the refrigerator and place them in the egg and milk mixture, swish them around to coat well and let them sit for a minute or two. Remove the shrimp one at a time and place them in the flour, coating each well. Shake off excess flour before placing the shrimp in the heated oil. Fry the shrimp until light or golden brown on each side. Remove the fried shrimp and place them on a paper towel to drain the excess oil.

In a small bowl, combine the mayonnaise and mustard. Spread both slices of bread with the mayonnaise and mustard mixture, then place a piece of lettuce on one or both slices of bread, add a slice or two of ripe tomato, and top off with shrimp. Place the other slice of bread on top. Cut in half or get a good grip. Take a big bite and love the goodness.

Fried Soft-Shell Crab Sandwich

Makes 2 sandwiches.

1 cup oil
2–4 soft-shell crabs
salt and black pepper for seasoning crabs
garlic powder for seasoning crabs
½ cup milk (whole or skim)
2 eggs, beaten
flour for coating crabs

Sauce
1 teaspoon mayonnaise
1 teaspoon mustard
2 dashes garlic powder
1–2 dashes hot sauce, optional

For Each Sandwich
2 slices bread
1–2 pieces lettuce
1–2 slices tomato, optional

Heat the oil in a skillet over medium heat. Rinse the soft-shell crabs under running water and let drain. Season the crabs to taste with salt, black pepper, and garlic powder. Put the flour in a bowl or paper bag. In a bowl, mix the milk and eggs. Place the crabs in the milk and egg mixture and toss until coated. Place them in the bowl or bag with the flour and shake or toss, coating the crabs well. Remove one crab at a time from the flour and place them in the hot oil. Let them fry until golden brown on both sides. When done, remove the crabs and place them on a paper towel to drain the excess oil.

In a small bowl, mix the sauce ingredients. Spread both slices of bread with the sauce; layer lettuce, tomato (if you like), and soft-shell crab. Top with bread and have yourself a delight.

Open-Face Crabmeat Sandwich

Makes 2–3 sandwiches.

¼ cup oil
½ pound crabmeat, white and claw
½ medium-sized onion, diced
¼ medium-sized green bell pepper, diced
¼ medium-sized red bell pepper, diced
pinch dried thyme
salt and black pepper for seasoning crabmeat
1 slice bread per sandwich

Sauce
1 teaspoon mayonnaise
1 teaspoon mustard
2 dashes garlic powder

Heat the oil in a skillet. In a bowl, mix the crabmeat, onion, green and red bell peppers, thyme, and salt and pepper to taste. Place the crabmeat mixture in the hot oil and let fry to the texture you desire. Remove the crabmeat and drain the excess oil on a paper towel. Combine the sauce ingredients and spread on a slice of bread; add cooked crabmeat on top of the bread. Cut into bite-sized portions to eat.

Baked or Broiled Fish Sandwich

Makes 2 sandwiches.

2–3 medium fillets of fish, your choice, clean and damp dried
1 teaspoon garlic powder
salt and black pepper to taste
½ teaspoon paprika

vegetable oil cooking spray
½ onion, sliced in rings
4 slices bread

For Broiling
2–3 tablespoons lemon juice
½ cup water

Combine the garlic powder, salt, pepper, and paprika and sprinkle them evenly on both sides of the fish fillets.

If you are baking the fish, lightly coat a baking pan with cooking spray, place the fish in the pan, and place the onion rings over and around the fish. Place the fish in a preheated oven at 350° and let bake for about 15 to 20 minutes — the cooking time will depend on the thickness of the fish and how done you like it. As soon as the fish is ready, remove it from the hot pan; otherwise it will continue to cook.

If you want to broil the fish, preheat the broiler in your oven. Place the fish in a pan coated with cooking spray. Place the onion rings over and around the fish and pour the lemon juice and water over the fish and onions. Cover the pan with foil, then place it in the oven and let the fish cook until done, about 15 to 20 minutes, or to your preferred taste. Do not overcook the fish or it will be too dry.

Put the tasty fish between 2 slices of bread and enjoy.

Fried Oyster Sandwich

Makes 2 sandwiches. Hello, oyster lovers!

½–1 pound oysters
1 cup oil
⅔ cup flour
½ teaspoon salt
½ teaspoon black pepper
½ teaspoon garlic powder

2 large eggs
⅔ cup whole milk
2–4 pieces lettuce
4 slices tomato
4 slices bread
sandwich spread—whatever kind you like

Drain the oysters well. Heat the oil in a medium or large skillet on me-dium high heat. In a bowl, combine the flour, salt, black pepper, and garlic powder. In a second bowl, beat the eggs, then add the milk and mix to-gether. Add the oysters to the milk and egg mixture and coat well. Remove them and place them in the flour mixture. Coat the oysters well and shake off any excess flour. Place the oysters in the hot oil and fry them until they are lightly brown, or to the level of crispiness you prefer. Oysters do not take long to cook, so please watch closely. You may fry your oysters crispy or soft. When oysters are fried hard, they shrink more. Remove the oysters and place them on a paper towel to absorb the excess oil. Put your favorite sandwich spread on 2 slices of bread, add lettuce and tomato, then stack on as many oysters as you like and dig in.

Soups

Soups were part of our diet several times a week. As soon as we children left for school, Momma or Pop would put on a long pot of bean soup, pea soup, or beef stew. We called this a "long pot" because it cooked all day long on the woodstove while we were at school—we didn't have crock pots then—and when we came home, the soup would be ready for us as a late lunch.

Momma and Pop were as good at making soups as they were at every-thing else they made. And they were both great cooks; I remember the evenings of their competitions in the kitchen and conversations around the wood heater or dinner table, recalling the days of going into the woods to get wagonloads of wood pulled by our cow, Bobby. Pop cut piles of it, enough to last for two or three days.

These days I enjoy sitting alongside Momma's bed as we spend hours talking about life on Daufuskie and the many meals we shared and the good times we spent together in the kitchen fixing and mixing, sharing moments that are now memories. Momma often wishes she could wake up to the rooster crowing back on Daufuskie, where she could walk outside and pick up a rake or hoe for her garden, throw some cracked corn to her chickens as they gathered around her feet to feed, or even carry a bucket of slop to the oinking hogs in the pen. She also wishes she could go back to fishing at the public dock or down at the creek.

Momma is a great-grandmother of 14 and great-great-grandmother of 16. She says if she was able she'd "tak'em all to 'Fuskie to be wit." I can see her now hollering at them while they have fun running freely in the backyard, playing in the dirt, and chasing the animals.

Momma is no longer able to put on her favorite handmade apron and skip around the kitchen rattling pots and pans, sending wonderful aromas throughout the house. But I am able to do that, and I still depend on all that she knows.

Today we have the pleasure of cooking faster or slower to suit our schedules; nevertheless we know how we like our food to taste. Technology has given us the ability to cook while we leave the house to do many other things. The one thing it can't give us is how to share from the heart. Today I try to teach my kids how wonderful it is to bring joy to one's heart with good home cooking.

Whether you are a country, apron-wearing cook or a city, high-heel-stepping cook, share it and bring what you know to the table. And don't forget to do it the way your momma or grandmomma showed you.

Grandmomma's Chicken Noodle Soup

When I get in my car and drive from Savannah to Hilton Head to catch a boat over to my home on Daufuskie, I get happy! Going back home makes me happy because my memories never leave me. The boat ride helps put me in a soothing mood. I still love the feeling that I get when I take my shoes off and walk down a dirt road or path, places where we—my sisters, my friends, and I—spent many hours running with bare feet.

The memories of yesterday take me back to Grandmomma's house, remembering how many times we ran and chased each other there. Or the trouble we used to get into. I can almost hear our voices as we played with each other or chased a chicken around the coop so Grandmomma could make her favorite soup. Making good chicken soup is one thing, but raising a yardful of chickens and picking out the right one or two is something else.

Momma used to trade a hen or rooster with other island natives to mate with what they had. They said it made the breed of the chicken better and they would grow bigger. Momma was one of a few who loved her birds; she had a yard full of chicken, ducks, turkeys, geese, and guineas, and it was our job to help her take good care of every one of them.

At one time Momma even had a few chickens that laid blue and green eggs. My sisters and I wondered if the egg inside was going to be the same color as the eggshell outside, but to our surprise it wasn't. We used to like it when a chicken laid her eggs, because the hen would cackle, letting us know what she had done. After a hen had finished laying all of her eggs, she would be ready to hatch them so that she could have dibbies—baby chicks. Momma would have us help her gather the rest of the eggs in the big bowl that she kept in a safe cool place in the house.

Momma would take the eggs to the chicken coop where she would take a sharpened pencil and carefully make scratch marks around each egg. She would count out about two dozen for each setting hen and place the marked eggs in the nest of the chicken that was ready to set. Marking the eggs helped identify them just in case a hen that was laying and not setting found her way to the wrong nest.

The setting hen would sit on the eggs for five to six weeks before the baby chicks would break open the shells with their beaks, then wiggle out, all wet, before drying into a cute cuddly dibby. Sometimes one or two of the eggs would not hatch, but Momma always knew that this could happen. She said this is where the saying comes from that you should never count your chickens before they hatch.

Sometimes at night, when everyone was in bed, all of a sudden the chickens, ducks, and turkeys would cackle, quack, and gobble, making lots of noise and waking everyone up. Pop would yell for us to get up and go outside with a flashlight to see what was going on. Most of the time it would be a snake with a bellyful of eggs and the birds were trying to make it go away. Other times there would be an opossum trying to get across the chicken wire fence to catch a chicken for his meal.

We would yell out to Pop, letting him know why the chickens were restless. He would come running with his double-barreled shotgun to take care of the matter. When all of the excitement was over, we would be ready to go back to bed, hoping the rest of the night would be quiet.

1 whole chicken, cut up and deboned
⅓ cup oil
2 stalks celery, chopped
1 large onion, chopped
1 medium-sized green bell pepper, chopped
2 quarts chicken broth or water
1 teaspoon dried thyme
2 bay leaves (optional)
1 cup carrots, chopped
1½ cups uncooked noodles
salt and black pepper to taste

Wash the chicken and let it drain. You can remove the skin, but the oil from the skin helps give the soup more flavor. Place the chicken pieces in a large pot with the oil, 1 stalk celery, half the onion, and the bell pepper; cook for 5 minutes, stirring occasionally. Add the broth or water, thyme, bay leaves, and remaining celery stalk and onion; let cook for 25 to 30 minutes. Add the carrots and noodles; taste and add salt and pepper as desired. Let simmer or slow cook for about 30 minutes. Taste and add whatever seasoning you think you need. Cook some more or scoop into a bowl and enjoy.

NOON

'Fuskie Seafood Gumbo

My momma served up her home-cooked meals to many folks from far and near for years. She had a way of making a little bit stretch into a lot. Her love for cooking was her joy, and you could taste it with every bite. She could cook and set a table with the best belly-filling meals. Momma loved cooking for anyone that wanted to eat, and she always liked to see smiles on folks' faces when they were through. When friends, guests, or even strangers had a meal at her table, they knew they had eaten some of the best cooking to be found down South.

One of everyone's favorites was her famous okra gumbo; people just couldn't get enough of it. Momma is an okra lover herself, and she never let them down. On occasion she would add something different to change the flavor. She knew what a difference it would make to add seafood to her gumbo. I always enjoyed being in the kitchen with Momma. The only time I wanted out was when it came time for her to put the okra in her gumbo because I didn't like the smell; then she would remind me to leave the kitchen.

Momma's guests loved everything she placed on the table. Some would ask her how she made such a delicious meal as they raved about her gumbo. They would eat second and sometimes third helpings. Momma would wait to clear the table, smiling proudly, and say, "Oh dat wasn't nuttin' to fix. I jus' throw sumptin together wit' what I had."

Not being able to eat okra or stand the smell of it cooking is a birthmark for me, but for those of you who think it makes the best gumbo in the whole wide world, enjoy it. My blessing is with all of you, and I hope you eat enough each time you sit down, just like those who ate at my momma's table.

Disyah da way Momma show me.

2 pieces fatback bacon
2 pieces smoked neck bone
3 pieces fresh pig tail

2 quarts hot water

2 14½-ounce cans stewed tomatoes

2 tablespoons tomato paste

1 bay leaf

1 teaspoon dried thyme

2–3 cloves garlic, diced

1 stalk celery, diced

1 large onion, diced

1½ dozen littleneck clams

½–1 pound lump crabmeat

1 pound medium-large shrimp

3–4 cups okra, sliced

1½ teaspoons sugar

salt and black pepper to taste

Once you have gathered all of the ingredients, take out a large soup pot and place it over medium heat. First, fry the fatback bacon; when it is done, remove and set aside, leaving the rendered fat in the pot. Add the neck bone, pig tail, and hot water to the pot and let boil for about 30 minutes. Stir in the tomatoes, tomato paste, bay leaf, thyme, garlic, celery, onion, clams, and fatback bacon. Let this cook for about 30 to 40 minutes, stirring occasionally. The soup should begin to thicken. Add the crabmeat, shrimp, okra, and sugar, plus salt and pepper to taste. Let this cook for about 20 to 30 minutes, stirring occasionally. If the soup gets too thick and you need to add more water, make sure it is hot.

Island Shrimp Creole

Folks like me just can't eat enough shrimp, no matter how you fix 'em. I am a shrimp lover and hope you are, too.

When Pop used to sit in his favorite chair knitting on his shrimp and mullet nets, he would sometimes whistle a familiar tune, usually a church song that he loved. It was a real treat for us to learn his favorite skill, but there was something better on our mind, like running around outside as much as possible.

Knitting a cast net took a lot of time, patience, and close attention. Knitting his cast nets was as good as gold for Pop. When he picked up his knitting needle and yarn, it was all he needed for the moment. Sometimes, after hours of knitting, one of the wooden needles would break. Pop would stamp his feet and shout out a bad word. He would go into the woods the following day and look for the right size tree to cut down. Using a tool called a shaver, he would shave a piece of wood into shape. We were always his assistants holding the wood steady. Once the wood was shaved, he would use his pocket knife to patiently carve a new knitting needle or two so he could finish the job.

Shrimp Creole wasn't what Momma called this dish, but she made it almost the same way. She just called it shrimp stew.

½ cup oil
1 large onion, cut in medium wedges
1½ stalks celery, chopped
1 large green bell pepper, chopped
1 large red bell pepper, chopped
1 14½-ounce can whole or stewed tomatoes
1 6-ounce can tomato sauce
2 bay leaves
2–3 cups hot water
salt and black pepper
2 pounds shrimp, peeled and deveined
½ teaspoon sugar

Heat the oil in a large pot over medium heat; add the onion, celery, and bell peppers. Sauté for 2 to 3 minutes. Add the tomatoes, tomato sauce, bay leaves, and water. Stir, then add salt and pepper to taste. Let boil for 30 to 45 minutes; turn down heat and let simmer on low for an additional 30 to 45 minutes. Add the shrimp and sugar about halfway through the simmering process. You can spice this up with a bit of hot sauce or hot pepper if you like, but be careful how much you add. It's great alone, but it is also good over rice, potatoes, or noodles.

Easy Vegetable Soup

Even though we children had to eat all of the vegetables on our plates, we didn't complain. Pop was strict with us about eating what was on our plates or going without. Our vegetables were always cooked tender, not left crunchy. Momma would do her best to make them taste good to us. She would always remind us that vegetables were good and would help make us strong if we ate enough.

All of our vegetables were homegrown. We were eating organic long before it was a trend. To help keep the bugs away we used cool ashes from the woodstove and heater. Our soil was treated with chicken, horse, pig, or cow manure—all natural. The manure did not have a pleasant scent, but it certainly helped make the vegetables bigger.

We didn't grow some vegetables—like broccoli, cauliflower, and eggplant—because Pop and Momma didn't care for them. Momma would plant a few beets every now and then. I like these vegetables and cook them as often as I can. You can add your favorite vegetables to this soup and have a good time.

2–3 pieces fatback bacon or smoked ham
1 large onion, diced
8–10 cups chicken broth or water
1½ cups frozen or fresh green beans, limas, or butter beans
1½ cups frozen or fresh whole-kernel corn
1½ cups frozen or fresh sweet peas
1½ cups frozen or fresh diced carrots
1 teaspoon dried thyme
1 teaspoon or more crushed garlic
1 cup frozen or fresh chopped broccoli (optional)
1–2 bay leaves
salt and black pepper to taste

In a large pot, fry the fatback bacon. Add the onion and cook for a couple of minutes. Add the broth, beans, corn, peas, carrots, thyme, and garlic.

Let cook on medium heat for 45 minutes. Stir, then add the broccoli and bay leaves. Add salt and pepper to taste. Cook for another 30 minutes, or until the beans are tender. You can add potatoes if you like a thicker soup.

Cabbage Soup

1 head cabbage
3 slices smoked bacon
2–3 cups hot water
salt and black pepper to season.

Cut the cabbage into quarters and then cut each quarter in half. Wash the cabbage under running water. Place in a colander to drain well. Fry the bacon in a medium-sized pot; add the drained cabbage to the pot. Be careful while doing this because the hot grease from the bacon will splatter and could burn you. Stir-fry the cabbage for about 1 to 2 minutes, then add the water and salt and pepper to taste. Let cook on medium heat until the cabbage is as tender as you desire.

Carolina Chili

When you think of eating chili, most times it's when the weather is cool. But eating chili can be good all year round, whether you like your chili with beans or ground meat, hot or mild. As with most soups today, it is easier for us to put it all in a crock pot and be on our merry way. Here is one way that I like to cook up a big pot of good chili. Some like it with beef; I like it with beef and pork. This is a real treat.

Disyah da way fa do it.

2 pounds lean ground beef
1 pound lean ground pork

3½ cups onion, chopped

1½ heaping tablespoons garlic, minced

⅓ cup green bell pepper, chopped

⅓ cup red bell pepper, chopped

3 tablespoons chili powder

4½ cups fresh tomatoes, diced

¾ cup tomato paste

1 teaspoon ground cumin

2 bay leaves

black pepper

⅔ teaspoon dried oregano

4 cups red kidney beans (optional)

1½ cups shredded cheddar cheese

In a large soup pot, brown the ground beef and pork. Add the onion, garlic, and bell peppers. Cook over medium heat until tender. Add the chili powder, tomatoes, tomato paste, cumin, bay leaves, black pepper, and oregano. Mix well and let simmer slowly for 1½ to 2 hours, stirring occasionally. You may add kidney beans at this time and cook for another 30 to 40 minutes. Stir in the cheese. Turn off the heat and dish up a bowlful of some belly-filling chili.

Yondah Black-Eyed Pea Soup

Black-eyed pea soup has always been one of my favorites, and Momma would cook it up for me whenever I asked. She knew that we didn't ask for much.

Before Grandmomma or Momma would put their beans or peas in water to soak, they would pick through them. I used to love putting the peas in a bowl and picking out the bad ones. I would race off to the front porch, hoping to find the swing empty. Then I would climb up, get comfortable, and hold my head down in the bowl to find all the bad peas and throw them away. Momma would usually give us about 30 minutes to do this job while she got other things ready in the kitchen. We would bring in the bowl of peas, and she would add them to the meat. But she would check to make sure that we got all the bad ones.

I like the smell of a pot of pea soup cooking even now. Your can substitute beef if you don't eat pork, and it will taste just as good.

3 pieces smoked bacon
3 pieces smoked neck bone
3 pieces fresh pig tail
1 piece ham hock or smoked ham
1 package (16 ounces) black-eyed peas

In a medium pot, fry the bacon. Remove the bacon and drain the grease and set aside. Fill the same pot two-thirds full of warm to hot water. Add all the other meat and let boil for about an hour, or until foam from the meat appears. Drain and rinse the meat under running water. Return the meat to the pot. Fill the pot about two-thirds full of water again and let come to a boil.

Meanwhile, put the black-eyed peas in a bowl. Unless you had someone else do this earlier (or you just aren't bothered by bad peas), look through them, picking out the bad ones—those that are cracked, black, halved, or odd in some way. Add water to the peas; some will float to the top of the bowl. Drain off the floating peas; add more water and drain again. Add the black-eyed peas and bacon to the meat in the pot and let cook until the peas are tender. Stir occasionally to keep the peas from sticking.

As the black-eyed peas cook and the liquid gets low or thick, add more hot water and stir. When the peas are done, you should have a nice, rich, medium-thick soup.

Specialties

During the winter, the daylight hours were shorter, but our routine with school and household chores remained about the same. By spring, everyone was ready for the cold weather to go away. My sisters and I had to keep warm clothing on while waiting patiently for warm weather to arrive.

While Momma loved spending the days of the cooler months in the house cooking, cleaning, or mending, she liked nothing more than opening up the doors and windows and letting the fresh air in when it began to warm up. Hugging the heater during the winter months was cozy, but it didn't take the place of being able to roam around outside. Of course, when the weather started to warm up, the biting bugs came along. If we wanted to sit outside during the late afternoons, Momma would light a smoke pot to keep the biting bugs and gnats away.

In the early spring, Pop and Momma couldn't get their minds off grabbing their garden tools and getting to work in the field. Both of them relied on their instinct and their knowledge and the *Old Farmer's Almanac* when it was time to start turning over the soil in the field at planting time. They often followed the phases of the moon to plant certain seeds nature's ways. A lot of times the tide played an important role also. Almost every household had an Almanac to help make certain decisions, right down to the best time to cut their hogs and cows and to plant their tadas.

Creamy Garlic Butter Mashed Tadas

4 large white potatoes
dash of salt
1–2 tablespoons butter or margarine
1–2 tablespoons garlic juice or minced garlic
3–4 tablespoons Carnation evaporated milk
bacon bits (optional)

Peel the potatoes and cut them into ½- to 1-inch-thick slices. Place them in a large pot half full of water and add the salt. Bring to a boil and let the potatoes cook until they are soft enough to be easily pierced with a fork. Drain the potatoes and place them in a large mixing bowl. Use a fork to mash the potatoes down, then add the butter and garlic. Using an electric mixer, slowly add the milk until well blended, then beat on medium or high speed for 2 minutes or more. Serve this up as it is, or add some bacon bits for more flavor.

Garlic Home Fries

1½ cups oil
4–6 large white potatoes, cut in ¼-inch wedges
2 tablespoons garlic powder or garlic juice
salt and black pepper to taste

Heat the oil in a large skillet while preparing the potatoes. Wash and drain the potatoes and damp dry with a paper towel or cotton cloth. Toss the potatoes with the garlic powder or juice to season. Place them in the refrigerator for 5 to 10 minutes before adding them to the hot oil. Be careful while adding the potatoes to the oil. Let the potatoes cook until brown on all sides, turning them as needed. Remove them from the pan and place on paper towels to drain excess oil. Season with salt and pepper.

Homemade Meatballs

2 pounds lean ground round
1 tablespoon salt
1 tablespoon black pepper
1 large onion, diced small
1 large green bell pepper, diced small
½ cup ketchup
⅔–1 cup bread crumbs
2 teaspoons crushed garlic or garlic powder
4–5 large eggs, beaten
2 tablespoons brown sugar

Keep the ground round chilled until ready to use, especially in warm weather. Place it in a bowl and add the salt, black pepper, onion, and bell pepper; then add the ketchup, bread crumbs, and garlic. In a separate bowl, mix the eggs and sugar together. Add them to the ground beef mixture and use your hands to combine everything well. Roll portions of the mixture around in your hand to shape into balls no larger than golf balls. Place as many as you can on a cookie sheet or baking pan without letting them touch. Bake at 375° for 10 to 15 minutes, or until done.

Sallie's Seafood Spaghetti

Pull out your best large pot and let's get cooking!

12–16 ounces of uncooked spaghetti
1 stick butter or margarine
¼ cup vegetable oil
½ pound lump crabmeat
½ pound small clams
½ pound oysters
1 medium-sized onion, diced small
1 teaspoon garlic powder
1 medium-sized green bell pepper, diced
1 medium-sized red bell pepper, diced
1–2 14½-ounce cans stewed tomatoes
1 tablespoon tomato paste
1 14½-ounce can chicken broth or water
1 tablespoon garlic, minced
1 teaspoon dried oregano (optional)
2 teaspoon dried basil (optional)
½ cup grated sharp cheddar cheese, more or less to taste
1 pound shrimp, peeled and deveined

While you are preparing the other ingredients, bring a large pot of water one-half to two-thirds full to a boil for cooking the spaghetti. Place the butter and oil in another large pot on medium heat. When the oil is hot, add the crabmeat, clams, oysters, onion, garlic, and bell peppers. Stir together for a good minute or two, then add the stewed tomatoes, tomato paste, chicken broth, garlic, oregano, basil, and grated cheese. Stir the mixture together and let it cook until the sauce begins to thicken. Add the shrimp and let cook for about 15 to 20 minutes more. At this time, place the spaghetti in the pot of boiling water and cook until it is as soft as you like it.

Check the sauce for the right thickness while the spaghetti is cooking. Remove the spaghetti from the hot water and drain. There are two ways to fix this dish: you can remove the spaghetti from the pot a little before it's done, combine it with the sauce, and let the sauce cook until the spaghetti is done, or you can cook the spaghetti well and serve the sauce over it.

Homemade Cheese Biscuits

Makes 1–1½ dozen.

2 cups all-purpose flour
1 tablespoon baking powder
1 teaspoon salt
5 teaspoons Crisco
¼ cup whole milk
2 eggs, beaten
heaping ⅔ cup of grated sharp cheese
¼ cup Parmesan cheese
½ stick margarine

In a large bowl, sift together the flour, baking powder, and salt. Add the Crisco, milk, eggs, sharp cheese, Parmesan cheese, and margarine. Combine the ingredients to form a dough and knead until soft and well mixed. Using a rolling pin, spread the dough to about ¼ or ½ inch thick. Cut the dough with a biscuit cutter (re-form the scraps and cut again until all the dough is used). Let bake in a preheated oven at 350° until the biscuits turn golden brown, about 20 to 30 minutes. Remove from the oven, let cool, and enjoy.

Ham and Tada Salad

Whether you have freshly baked, just-out-of-the-oven ham or leftover ham, this is a great meat-and-potato salad that will feed your beenyah or comeyah soul.

6–8 medium potatoes (red or white), with or without skins, diced
1–1½ pounds baked ham, diced
1 small onion, diced
½ medium-sized green bell pepper, diced
½ medium-sized red bell pepper, diced
1 teaspoon black pepper
1 tablespoon pimentos (optional)
2 tablespoons sweet pickle relish or cubes
5–6 hard-boiled eggs, chopped
⅔ cup mayonnaise

In a large pot of water, cook the potatoes until they are tender enough to be pierced easily with a fork. Drain and let cool if you like. Add the ham, onion, bell peppers, black pepper, pimentos, sweet cubes, and eggs. Toss together, then add the mayonnaise and lightly combine. Now serve it up.

Chicken Coop Egg Salad

My grandmomma once had a rooster that was as protective as a watchdog and as mean as a rattlesnake. Even though it didn't bark or crawl on its belly, it cackled and picked at you; its long spurs would hurt you. If you went to Grandmomma's house and were not an everyday visitor, the rooster would not allow you to enter the gate to the house. The rooster would prance back and forth by the gate making noise when it saw you coming. This rooster proudly defended his territory, as if he was saying, "You can't come in this yard."

When Grandmomma heard the rooster making a fuss, she knew some-one was at the gate. She would have to come out of the house, meet her visitors at the gate, and walk them into the house shooing the bird away. This rooster didn't like kids either, but we knew to get a big stick and scare it away from our legs before it tried pecking on us.

Momma made sure we always had lots of fresh chicken eggs by having a yardful of chickens. Half of our chickens were for laying and hatching eggs for new chickens. Our "chickens" were a mixture of roosters, ducks, geese, turkeys, and guineas. Momma even had some frizzy chickens that were ugly to us kids, but Momma loved them all.

8 hard-boiled eggs
½ teaspoon garlic powder
½ teaspoon black pepper
pinch salt
1–1½ tablespoons sweet pickle relish or cubes
⅓ cup mayonnaise
½ teaspoon paprika

Run cool water over the eggs after they have boiled so they will be cool enough to handle. Peel and dice the eggs and place them in a medium-sized mixing bowl. Add the garlic powder, black pepper, salt, and relish; mix well. Add the mayonnaise and paprika. Spread on your favorite bread and bite in.

Daufuskie-Way Deviled Eggs

1 dozen eggs
⅔ teaspoon salt
½ teaspoon black pepper
2 tablespoons mayonnaise
2–3 dashes hot sauce (optional)

½ teaspoon garlic juice (optional)
1½ tablespoons sweet pickle relish or cubes
paprika for garnish

Place the eggs in a large pot and add enough cold water to cover the eggs by about an inch. Bring to a boil and cook the eggs for 15 to 20 minutes. When the eggs are cooked, remove from the stove and drain. Run cool water over the eggs while you peel them. Carefully cut the eggs in half, lengthwise. Remove the yolk from each half and place in a bowl. Place egg white halves on a plate or platter. Use a fork to mash the yolks; add the remaining ingredients to the yolks. Use a spoon to combine well, then place the yolk mixture in a pastry bag and squeeze it out to fill each egg white half. Sprinkle paprika lightly over the eggs to give them a nice finish. Enjoy.

Homemade Wines

By the time the last bit of homemade wine was about to be drunk, it was time to make up a whole new batch. Making homemade wine took good taste buds, practice, and patience, because no wine was good before it fermented to perfection. Momma and Pop, like other folks on the island who made the tasty drink, would make up gallons of their wine. It was made with southern love and a kind of wild southern feeling.

I recall my parents' patience as they would count down the weeks after placing the preparations in their containers. Their next step would be a taste test, and then they would make sure the wine was in a safe place to finish fermenting. Folks from all over liked the way 'Fuskie Island wine was made from natural fruit or berry juice with just enough sugar and water, and with no additives, substitutes, or preservatives. Most of all it had a lot of tasting before it passed the taste test. White sugar was added to help pump up the flavor and bring out the strength, because the sweeter the berry, the better the flavor and color.

Pop and Momma would prepare 3 to 5 five-gallon containers of each flavor they made. Momma made sure that, long before the wine was ready, we girls collected as many pint and half-pint bottles as we could find. They would fill those bottles from the fermenting jugs when the wine was ready.

Making homemade wine is an easy but slow process. It takes skill to know the right consistency and taste for each wine. Overprocessing can make the wine sour and tart, but if it is not processed long enough, with the right amount of sugar, then it can be bitter, and it will not taste right.

It has been said that island folks "sho'nuff" know how to make the best homemade wine. 'Fuskie folks brewing it right goes back many generations. Pop and Momma could not resist telling us stories about how their parents did it certain ways.

The wine was always made with natural juices that made it potent, allowing you to feel real good and mellow. Some folks knew how to handle their drinking, whereas some folks just liked the way it made them feel.

Friends from across the way on the mainland still talk about the good times they had riding Captain Sam's boats over to Daufuskie, when having fun felt like rejoicing; they recall the times of getting together with friends and family and eating the best seafood cooked by the islanders. It was often the only time they got to visit the folks that they knew from the island. They would recall the great food and the good drink. Many tall tales have been told about days sitting under the oak or mulberry trees, and many truths were loosened from the tongues of island folks while they chugged down a few cups or glasses of homemade wine. The conversation always got longer and louder with each glass they drank.

If you have not tasted 'Fuskie homemade wine, you just might be missing out on a real treat and a taste you'll always remember. If you like good wines made naturally, then see if you can master the Daufuskie way.

TIP: In making homemade wine, never stir the sugar when you add it to the fruit in order for it to ferment as expected.

'Fuskie Backyard Pear Wine

Add these ingredients to a 5-gallon jug or plastic container and let them do their own thing.

sliced pears (leave peels on)
4 pounds sugar
water

Slice enough pears to fill a 5-gallon jug about two-thirds full; add the sugar and let ferment in a medium-dark area for 5 to 7 days. Add cold water to within about 2 inches of the top of the container. Cover with a slightly loose top or a piece of cotton cloth fastened with a tie or rubber band to hold it in place. Put the container back in the medium-dark area for 4 to 5 weeks.

When this time has passed, make sure the sugar is mixed in well by stirring the concoction or shaking the container, and give the wine a taste. Stir again and add more sugar if needed. Let sit for 2 to 3 weeks more, and taste again. If it meets your taste buds' approval, strain the residue from the wine using a clean white cotton cloth or fine strainer. Continue to strain until the wine is clear. Rinse the jug used to ferment the wine and return the home-made wine to that same jug until it is time to pour it into smaller containers for measuring or just to have a good drink of your homemade treat.

Orchard Plum Wine

It seems as if it was just yesterday when Momma would announce, "It's plum picking time." Momma and Pop knew that they had to keep an eye on us children more during the hot days of summer because there was much more trouble for us to get into. As the weather heated up and the berries and fruits ripened, we knew it was near time to pick the plump plums that draped the trees as we watched them turn colors from green to yellow and then red.

Without going too far out of our way, we could find the trees with the most fruit. But we were not the only ones who loved the juicy plums; birds, deer, and other animals wanted to get their share, too, so we had to get to the plums before they did.

My sisters and I, along with about half the other island kids, were happy when we saw a plum tree drooping with plums along the roadside. We knew our parents would let us pick as many plums as we could bring home. Going into the plum orchard was not something they did. A few of us would plan a meeting place with our closest friends or nearest relatives, and by the next day there would be a big group of us. Daufuskie had a grape-vine that worked as well as any telephone.

We kids would have our foot tubs and buckets ready to go the day be-fore. At times like this, we would make a game of seeing who could fill their buckets up first, but tag and hide-and-seek were always more fun. The day would be filled with work and play, depending on how many plums we picked. It was always fun getting together to enjoy each other's company, even just for gathering plums.

Our parents would remind us to be very careful and to look out for snakes. The only problem with that was, the snakes had to look out for us as we came tramping through the thick trees. As kids we didn't care where we stepped or what we stepped on. We were too busy running from one tree to the next, chasing each other around the thick, thorny trees, filling our bellies as we picked the sweet, juicy plums.

Looking back on those days, I don't know how we avoided getting bitten by some of the poisonous snakes and big spiders that lived on the island. We had no fear of all the danger that was around us. Pop used to tell us that God looks out for fools and babies. The woods on Daufuskie were our playground, and we ruled our kingdom as we roamed freely through it all, whether we were about work or play. Danger lurked all around, but all we cared about was where our imaginations took us on our many adventures, whether we were swinging from the big grapevines or climbing the tallest tree. Surely the snakes knew that they needed to get out of our way and fast.

As we tired of play, we got to eat our fill of many juicy plums before going home to our parents' watchful eyes. Sometimes we paid for eating too much, but with all the fun we had, it was well worth it.

Our parents didn't mind us going into the woods as long as we behaved and brought back what we went to get. Besides Momma and Pop using plums to make their homemade wine, we could sell them at the boat rides on weekends. A big boat carrying 200–300 people would come from Savannah and folks would buy bags of plums, plus the wonderful seafood and other goodies our parents had prepared for them: famous Daufuskie deviled crabs, hot boiled crabs and shrimp, good homemade wine, and peanuts and pecans in season. Selling our plums gave us money for school clothes for the next year. Momma and Pop always made us realize that we had to work for what we wanted.

4–5 pounds ripe plums
4–5 pounds sugar
1 gallon water per 1 pound of plums

Place the plums, sugar, and water in a 5-gallon glass or plastic container and cover the container loosely. Place the container in a closed, dark area. Let sit for 2 to 3 weeks. Stir and taste; add more sugar if needed, then let sit for 3 to 4 more weeks. Strain several times and pour into clean containers for storing or serving.

Persimmon Wine

My sisters and I used to like climbing all kinds of trees, but our parents did not want us to climb fruit trees. Pop would say, "It's bad luck fo' girls ta get up dem fruit trees." We didn't understand why only girls were forbidden to climb a fruit tree, so we asked. Pop always explained that the fruit trees would not bear the following year. He said, "Girl churn grow up ta be 'oh-man. 'Oh-man have churn, like da fruit tree has fruits." For that reason a woman is not supposed to climb up a tree. Well, we never told them what they did not see.

As I recall, we used to have several big persimmon trees that hung over a pasture fence across the road near the house. Persimmons were not one of our favorite fruits. Pop and Momma loved the fact that we wouldn't eat more than we picked for their homemade wine. Persimmons were not known for making meals on Daufuskie, just for making really good wine.

ripe and overripe persimmons
10 pounds sugar, more or less, divided
water

Fill a 5-gallon plastic or glass container about one-third full of ripe and overripe persimmons. Add water to within about 3 inches of the top. Add about 5 pounds of the sugar. Cover loosely with a lid, and place in a dark, out-of-the-way area for about 3 weeks. After that time, check the smell—it should be a strong robust scent, not a sour fume—and taste, and add another 5 pounds or more of sugar to achieve the desired consistency and strength. Stir lightly and place back in a dark area for 2 more weeks.

After 2 weeks remove, check for taste and consistency again, and strain the wine by squeezing all the juice from the the persimmons through cheesecloth or cotton cloth. Rinse out the container and pour the strained wine back into it unless you have another container you want to store it in. Serve with or without ice for a dandy taste. Making any homemade wine is always up to the maker's taste buds. It is important to taste for strength and sweetness when testing for flavor. A good homemade wine is perfected by its maker.

Backyard Mulberry Wine

Mulberry trees are strong, with long branches, and they grew all over the island. Most islanders had a mulberry tree, big or small, in their front yard or back. We had a great big one, and it was the center of attention; it was like an entertainment center in the backyard. As a matter of fact, we had many uses for it year-round.

Pop knew that we needed a safe play area close to the house, so he made a swing for us and hung it in the mulberry. It was made with the strong rope that was used to tie the cow and the horse in the field when they grazed there; the seat was a piece of wooden board. We would often play under the tree on hot summer days. "Here We Go 'Round the Mulberry Bush" was our song.

The shade of the big mulberry tree was the coolest place to sit and relax when the house was too hot, especially when Momma was cooking. Some-times Momma would wash clothes under it when the sun was too hot near the house. And on hot summer days when the sun took over the porch as well as the house, Pop and his friends would gather underneath the mulberry tree to drink their moonshine or their homemade wine and tell their folktales.

Pop would hang the hog from the mulberry tree during hog-killing time. We even had our woodpile nearby, where we would cut wood out of the sun for the woodstove and heater. Pop had built benches under the tree for everyone to sit on. It must have loved the attention and conversation we gave it through the years.

First it would have leaves, then blooms, then berries. The berries started out green, but as they grew, they turned red and then dark bluish purple. At the berries ripened, they would finally become sweet and juicy.

We would eat so many berries that our hands and mouths turned dark blue; this was fun to us kids, even though Momma didn't think so. We would get the dye from the berries in our clothes and it was hard for her to wash it out. As much as my sisters and I loved to eat the sweet, juicy berries, we were not allowed to climb the tree to get to the berries high above.

Every year our mulberry tree would hang with these sweet berries droop-ing from the limbs. Momma and Pop would be happy, because this meant they were going to make lots of homemade wine. When the berries were ripe, they would start falling, and Pop would have us put down canvas or anything that would catch the berries before they touched the ground; if they got sand on them, it was difficult to wash off.

We would all gather under the tree, picking and eating by the handfuls, filling up. Momma would sometimes yell, "Dontcha eat dem berries! Din-nah be ready soon." She knew that we would eat too much and we would not want dinner. Momma and Pop knew that no matter how hard they tried to scold us for doing the wrong thing, we just sometimes had to find out the hard way and pay the price for not listening.

When they left the house, they would warn us not to eat any more mul-berries while they were gone. We would sneak under the mulberry tree anyway, thinking they would not find out, but on their return our mouths would be colored from the berries. No matter how hard we tried, we could not wash off the dark color of the mulberries. Sometimes we would eat more than our stomachs could hold and then get a bad stomachache. Pop would look at us and laugh, as we would be bending over, holding our stomachs, crying from the pain after eating too many mulberries.

He would walk over to the cupboard and pull out the big bottle of cas-tor oil and a large tablespoon. Our heads would turn away because this was one medicine we didn't like at all. Pop would remind us, "Hard heads make soft behinds. Line up 'cause ya didn't listen; disyah whatcha get." Sometimes this was worse than getting a spanking.

When the lower berries were all gone and we couldn't reach the higher ones, Momma and Pop would have us get a long stick with a "Y" shape at the top so that we could "trash" the tree: we would place the "Y" of the stick under a limb of the tree and shake it well until the berries came falling down on the canvas. Sometimes we would throw sticks up in the tree to knock the berries down, but we had to watch where the sticks landed—not on our heads. When we got through picking up as much as Momma and Pop needed, they would turn the hogs and chickens out to eat the rest of the berries.

mulberries

3–4 gallons water

5 pounds sugar, more or less

After picking enough mulberries to fill a 5-gallon glass or plastic container two-thirds full, lightly rinse them with water; be gentle, as they bruise easily. Place them in the container. Add the water, pour in the sugar, and let sit in a dark area for 2 to 3 days with a loosely fitted lid. When that time is up, taste and pour in more water if the win is too strong. Replace the lid, place in a dark area, and let sit for 3 to 4 weeks before checking.

You can tell if it is seeping (beads of air are foaming from the wine) to perfection. Stir to incorporate any undissolved sugar, and taste to see if you need to add more. Set aside for a couple more weeks. If the strength is to your taste, it will be time to strain the liquid from the berries.

Momma used to use part of an old white sheet to strain wine. You can pour the strained wine into a different container or back into the container it was made in if it has been cleaned or rinsed well. Now it's sipping time: pour yourself a glass, sit on your porch or under a tree, and enjoy. The wine will taste better as it ages.

'Fuskie Peach Wine

Fruit trees grew well on Daufuskie, and peach trees were no exception. The only problem was that they produced much smaller fruit than the peaches we got from the grocery store. But size was not a factor when it came to making homemade peach wine. The important thing was that the tree had enough peaches for a good batch. Sometimes Momma and Pop got a basketful of bruised and mashed peaches from the fruit market in Savannah. On occasion the peaches were given to them just to get rid of them. They would happily bring the peaches home to make more gallons of this wine, because it was a favorite. We kids had to settle for the juicy peaches themselves and the sweet desserts they made, though, from time to time, if we had helped make the wine, Momma and Pop would give us a taste when it was ready.

5 pounds ripe and overripe peaches, rinsed and sliced (but not peeled)
3–4 pounds sugar
3–4 gallons water, room-temperature

Place the peaches in a 5-gallon plastic or glass container. Add the sugar and let sit for 2 to 3 days. Add the water and stir. Place a lid on top but do not seal tightly, or you can just place something over the jug to cover it well. This will keep bugs out while the wine is fermenting. Let sit for 4 to 5 weeks in a dark area. Stir and let settle before straining through a clean cloth. Place the wine in a clean glass or plastic container or containers, or return it to the container in which it fermented, after rinsing the container.

Roadside Blackberry Wine

Sweet, juicy blackberries grew wild all over Daufuskie Island. You could walk along most roadsides where the sun smiled down all day, and there would be patches of blackberries everywhere. The sticky bush that the blackberries grew on never stopped us from reaching in and getting stuck while pulling the berries off by the handful. All we knew and wanted was the sweet-tasting berries that dyed our mouths and hands and went into the good desserts Momma made. The blackberries didn't last too long because, besides us picking as many as we could, the birds and other creatures loved them too.

My sisters and I often picked blackberries for our grandaunts and some of the other elder folks on the island if they asked us to, and our reward would be about fifty cents for a bucketful. If we returned when they had made their sweet desserts, we would be invited to have some blackberry dumplings.

When making blackberry wine or any other homemade wine, it is very important that your product suits your taste. Everyone's taste buds differ, but we all like a good taste. Whether the wine smells the right way is something you have to judge yourself. What's important is that it not smell sour. If it does smell sour, that's usually the result of overprocessing, so check it more frequently to guard against overprocessing if you like. You will learn more as you go along.

blackberries
5 pounds sugar
water

Fill a 5-gallon plastic or glass container about two-thirds full of blackberries. Add water to within about 3 inches of top. Add the sugar and stir lightly. Cover loosely with a lid so that as the wine brews and strengthens it does not blow off the top, leaving a mess to clean up.

Place in a dark area and leave for 3 weeks. Remove and check for taste and consistency; if needed, add more sugar (some berries are sweet, and some are not). If the taste is not to your satisfaction, cover again, and place back in a dark area for about 2 more weeks.

Using a cheesecloth or white cotton cloth, strain the wine, squeezing as much juice from the berries as you can. Rinse the container and pour the strained wine back in or place in new containers as you prefer. Let the wine sit in a dark area until you are ready to serve it.

Grandmomma's Favorite Elderberry Wine

We don't hear too much about elderberries anymore. They grow in a bunch on a tree, and my grandmother had several big elderberry trees growing in her backyard. She loved to make her elderberry wine.

elderberries
4–5 pounds sugar
water

Carefully pick, wash, and drain enough elderberries to fill a 5-gallon plastic or glass container halfway. Place the berries in the container and then fill with water to within 3 inches of the top. Cover but do not seal tightly. Let sit in a dark, out-of-the-way area for 2 to 3 weeks. Then add the sugar. Stir, cover, and let sit for 3 to 4 more weeks. Check for taste and consistency. When the wine is ready, strain and pour into a glass or plastic container or containers or rinse the container in which it fermented and return the wine to that container. Serve at room temperature or chilled.

Drink responsibly, no matter who makes the brew.

Pleasing Drinks

Kool-Aid was and still is my favorite drink; we liked it better than soda pop. Momma loved fixing it by the big pitcherful, with thick slices of lemon from time to time. Today I still love all the many flavors of Kool-Aid, and I usually keep a pitcherful in the refrigerator.

The drinks we had were tasty and plentiful, and we enjoyed them all. We had fresh cow's milk, straight from our cow, Sarah. We had several kinds of teas that were good and healthy for us. But a cool glass of good old-fashioned lemonade would quench our thirst like nothing else. It goes without saying that we drank a lot of freshly pumped water; it was refreshing and cool, coming from the ground, no matter what the season.

Sometimes my sisters and I would make up drinks when our parents would let us use some sugar. Drinks like sugar and water or Carnation milk and water were tasty. Using sugar was a treat for us, and it was not to be taken advantage of. We grew a whole lot of sugarcane, but we used that for other things.

Ol' Country Lemonade with Orange

You've got to roll 'em, squeeze 'em, and cut 'em up.

Lemons and oranges together make a refreshing citrus drink that goes down great. We didn't have a lemon or orange tree in our backyard, but we surely loved to make and drink this combination whenever Momma brought these fruits home from her shopping. Momma would load up on lemons on her monthly trip to the mainland; she bought oranges mostly around Christmastime.

Lemons in our house were not just used for making lemonade; they were also used in some of Momma's home remedies and her good cooking.

If you'd like to give your lemonade a change of flavor, try adding some squeezed oranges, with or without the peel, for a tasty difference.

4 lemons, rolled, squeezed to extract the juice, and sliced thin
5 oranges, rolled, squeezed to extract the juice, and sliced thin
2 cups sugar, or more to taste
2 gallons water

Place the sliced lemons and oranges, along with the lemon and orange juices, in a 2-gallon container. Add the sugar and stir. Add the water and stir until the sugar is dissolved. Pour into a glass with ice and relax. You might serve this with a meal.

Fresh Mellow Mint Tea

Momma loved her fresh mint growing along with her pretty spring and summer flowers. You could walk by her flower garden and get a whiff of the sweet mint. It grew right alongside the front porch. Sometimes we would be sitting in the swing on the front porch, and a nice breeze would blow in the right direction to send the fresh scent of mint toward us. Momma often made this mint tea to drink for an upset stomach. We just liked it because it tasted and smelled so good. Boiling mint sends a great minty aroma throughout the house.

PICK A BUNCH of fresh mint—about a handful. Hold it under running water and shake the mint leaves to release any dirt or sand. Meanwhile, heat a medium pot half full of water. Break the mint plants in half and add to the hot water. Let boil for about 10 to 15 minutes. Remove and let sit for another 10 minutes. Pour a cupful and add a bit of honey, sugar, or nothing at all. Take a comfortable seat and enjoy each pleasing sip.

Soothing Sassafras Tea

Going into the woods or along the road to dig for sassafras was more fun than you can imagine. We couldn't wait to go down the road a bit with Pop to cut down the best sassafras tree; we would dig up the roots so that we could have a great-tasting sassafras tea by the wood heater on a cool winter night.

Pop would usually have us gather the ax, grubbing hoe (this hoe has a longer, narrower blade than a regular hoe), croaker sacks, and buckets. Momma would make sure we were bundled up; then off into the woods we would go to dig sassafras, which grows wild all over Daufuskie.

The tree has three types of leaves: the youngest leaf on the sassafras tree looks like a regular leaf, the next looks like a mitten, and the final stage of the leaf looks as if it has three fingers. You will see all three of these leaves on a tree as it matures. Even after a frost, the leaves stay on the tree for a while. You can also identify the tree by popping a branch and smelling it. It has a wonderful smell you'll love.

Pop would point out the size of tree we needed to cut down, and he would get his grubbing hoe and dig along the tree root. He was more experienced, and he wanted to teach us the right way to get all the roots from the ground. Instead of taking just a chunk out of the root, we would take as much of the root as possible. It was easier to extract the roots of the young trees from the ground. My sisters and I would grab hold of a root cut from the bottom of the tree and pull hard on it, pulling up the remainder of the root. Pop would take the ax and cut off the end of the root if it stuck in the ground.

It has been said by reliable sources—our parents—that you can dig the root of the sassafras tree only after the first frost in the fall. By then the sap would have fallen from the top to the bottom in the roots of the tree, which would make the root more potent and the tea taste better. Sassafras roots have three layers of colors: the outer layer is dark brown like the dirt it grows in; the second layer is dark pink or reddish; and the inside layer is cream colored.

We would gather the croaker sacks full of roots, wash them, and hang them to dry on the back porch. The sassafras root gives off a sweet aroma as it dries. Momma would have dinner cooking while we gathered the roots from the sassafras trees. This was usually an evening task because the woods would be dry, not wet from the morning dew.

Everyone that I knew on the island loved to drink sassafras tea all the time; for us it was the best. Sassafras tea was what we drank when others were drinking soft drinks. We would have a cup or two of sassafras tea and eat cornbread with syrup or whatever we had to go along with it. We would listen to stories while we had this evening refreshment, and this was our relaxing fun time, especially after a hard workday.

WASH A HANDFUL of roots, removing all the dirt that you can. You can either let the root dry for a few days or use it immediately. Break the roots into pieces to fit into a medium-large pot. Add enough water to cover roots by about 1 inch; let boil for 20 to 30 minutes on medium heat. Turn heat down to medium-low and let simmer a while longer if you like a stronger flavor. Pour yourself a cupful, add a little sugar or honey if you wish, and savor the aroma and the taste of a great tea that relaxes your whole body. You can reboil the roots; the flavor will thin out, but it will still be good.

Whether you are a morning, noon, or night tea drinker, try some sassafras tea with a chunk of cornbread or any bread you like; it will soothe your beenyah soul.

Orange Peel Tea

We got to drink this tea during the Christmas season. At that time of year Momma would set out oranges and some other fruit in a punch bowl on the dining room table. Surrounding it was Christmas candy and slices of cake. Even though we rarely got anything for Christmas besides new school clothes and shoes, we never complained.

Eating lots of fruit was OK with Momma and Pop. Peeling and eating the big, juicy oranges was fun for me and my sisters, as we would sometimes squirt the juice on one another. On occasion we would save the orange peels to boil for a tasty tea, though sneaking a little bit of sugar for the tea wasn't always easy. Sometimes our parents would be in a good mood and give us the OK to make the tea. After boiling the orange peels, we would strain the tea from the peels, which would have become soft and juicy. Eating the soft peels was fun, too. Making this tea was cheap and easy, and we loved it. Try boiling your orange peels and get a great tea drink from them.

peels from 2–3 medium-large oranges
water
sugar to taste

Before peeling the oranges, wash them well. Add the orange peels to a medium-sized pot half filled with room-temperature water and bring the water to a boil. Let boil for 10 to 15 minutes. Set aside to steep for 5 to 10 minutes. Pour the tea through a strainer into cups; add sugar or another sweetener of your choice. Sit back and enjoy the orange's bittersweet, second-time-around taste.

Country Hot Toddy

You know how a cold slowly eases up on you with a little scratchy throat and a sniffle here and there. Sometimes a little chill and fever will kick in, making you feel bad. Back on Daufuskie, at the first signs of a cold Momma would put on a pot of hot toddy; she did not like to wait for a cold to get too far. After we had finished all our outside work, eaten supper, and had a bath, Momma would give us a tin cup (a vegetable can) half full of hot toddy to drink right before we went to bed. The tin cup helped keep it hot enough to drink. We liked it with a little sugar, but Pop said it works better without.

"Off ta ya bed," Momma would say, "and get undah dem covahs" The toddy would not help if you didn't go right to bed. You could not get out of bed once you drank the toddy and had been tucked in for the night. Drinking the toddy and getting under a bundle of warm handmade quilts made us sweat out the cold that was trying to mature.

2–3 lemons, sliced or diced
1½ quarts water (half this amount if you want it stronger)
½ pint gin

Put the water and lemons in a pot and let them come to a boil. Turn the heat down just enough to keep the mixture hot. Add the gin, and let simmer for about 15 minutes more. Serve with fresh lemon pieces and go to bed.

Stuffin' It Full

Progress has changed a lot of things on Daufuskie—now there are golf courses, million-dollar houses, paved roads, stop signs, and limits on where you can go. All these things and more have come to Daufuskie. But none of these changes will ever erase the good times and close connections of the smaller community that we once had. Daufuskie is still a unique and beautiful island. Some wonderful folks have moved there and love the peaceful island as much as natives do.

Eating fresh seafood during my childhood on Daufuskie was a real joy, and that has not changed. You can still catch your own mullet from the mullet holes where Pop used to catch fish with his mullet nets. You can go down to the docks and set a trap with a chicken back or neck to catch some crabs, or you can throw a fishing line, baited with shrimp or fiddler crabs, and catch some whiting, corkers, catfish, and trout in season. And if you know how to throw a cast net, you can catch some shrimp, too.

Today, developers have created several manmade lakes, stocked with a variety of freshwater fish. Maybe during the right season you can still go to the beach and find some conchs buried halfway in the wet beach sand at low tide. If you love to eat oysters, you can put on some good rubber boots, go to an oyster bank when the tide is low, and pick as many oysters as you want. Remember to pick and eat them only in months that have an

"R" in their names, and be careful where you put your feet or you may get stuck in the mud.

If you know how to grow it, pick it, catch it, or hunt it, then living on Daufuskie is a great place—even without a store—because you will always have a meal to eat some way and somehow. I learned about being poor, but I also learned that what matters is what you do with what you have.

If you have a favorite meat and you want to stuff it full, fill it with a mixture of seafood or stuffing seasoned the way you like. You will enjoy the flavor of two great tastes coming together.

Flounder Full of Crabmeat

A flounder is a flat, slightly round, meaty, good-tasting fish. Like most fish, it has scales. The top side of a flounder is dark and the bottom is off-white. The flounder has one solid, flat bone, with fine bones in the fins. Flounder has a mild to medium-strong taste when cooked. You can bake, grill, stew, fry, or broil it, just as you can most other fish. To catch a flounder you have to bottom fish: you fish with the line baited and you let it touch the bottom, which is where flounder feed and live most of the time.

Flounder stuffed with crabmeat is very good. The two seafoods combined make a great meal, baked or broiled.

2 whole flounders, medium to large
salt and black pepper for seasoning

Crabmeat Stuffing
⅓–½ stick butter or margarine
½ medium-sized onion, diced
¼ medium-sized green bell pepper, diced
¼ medium-sized red bell pepper, diced
1 pound lump crabmeat
1 tablespoon sweet pickle relish or cubes
1 tablespoon mayonnaise
1 teaspoon mustard (optional)

1 clove garlic, crushed

2 pinches dried thyme (optional)

1 teaspoon salt

1 teaspoon black pepper

You can buy flounder filets at the supermarket or catch and clean your own fish. Here are some tips if you are cleaning the fish yourself.

Like all fish, flounder needs to be kept moist for scaling or else the scales will become dry, making them harder to remove. Place the fish in a pan or sink filled with cool or room-temperature water. Remove one fish at a time from the water and place it on a flat surface. Use a sharp knife to scale it and be careful.

I start at the tail and scrape upward toward the head with each stroke. This motion will release the scales from the skin most easily. You will find it helpful to dip the fish in the water a few times between scrapes, removing loose scales as you go.

Once you have scraped all the scales from both sides, including those on the head, you will need to open the fish up to remove the guts. A flounder doesn't have as much stomach as some fish, and it is located right near the head, not in the center, where you find the stomach on most fish.

When you have finished scaling, rinse the fish and look for a little hole not quite halfway down toward the tail on the off-white side. Cut from that point in a circular shape toward the head and detach the internal organs in the softer area. Remove the stomach and throw it away; then clean the fish well with running water. Turn the fish over, with the dark side facing up. Use a small but sharp knife. Depending on how large your fish is, make a horizontal cut about 3 to 4 inches right down the middle. Stay on top of the bone just as if you were filleting it, making a pocket on both sides. This is the area that you will stuff with the crabmeat.

Sprinkle the flounder lightly with salt and pepper. Cover the fish with a wet napkin or place it in a covered container (to help keep it moist) and put in the refrigerator while you make the crabmeat stuffing.

In a saucepan, melt the butter and sauté the onion and bell peppers for 2 to 3 minutes. Add these ingredients to the crabmeat in a bowl, along with the pickle relish or cubes, mayonnaise, mustard, garlic, thyme, and salt and pepper. Combine all the ingredients and taste to see whether you need to adjust the seasoning.

Remove the flounder from the refrigerator. Put 1 or 2 tablespoonfuls of crabmeat into the pocket of each flounder and pack well. Place the stuffed flounder on a pan that has been lightly greased or coated with cooking spray. Place in a preheated oven at 350° and bake 25 to 30 minutes, until both the fish and the crabmeat are slightly brown. Test for texture, making sure flounder is cooked enough for you. Remove from the oven—the rest is up to your mouth, your stomach, and your appetite.

Salmon Stuffed with Crabmeat and Shrimp

1 half side of a whole salmon fillet, skin on or not

Crabmeat and Shrimp Stuffing
½ pound lump crabmeat
½ pound small shrimp, peeled, deveined, and cooked
1 medium-sized onion, diced
½ medium-sized green bell pepper, diced
½ medium-sized red bell pepper, diced
1 teaspoon dried thyme
½ cup crushed Ritz crackers
⅓–½ cup mayonnaise

In a bowl, combine the crabmeat, shrimp, onion, bell peppers, thyme, and Ritz crackers. Add the mayonnaise. You can add more or less mayonnaise, but don't make the mixture soft; it needs to be firm. Spread the mixture on top of the salmon. Carefully roll the salmon up, starting at the tail. Stuff more seafood mixture in from the side if you can. Use toothpicks to hold the salmon together at the center and both ends. Placed the rolled, stuffed salmon in a baking pan lined with aluminum foil. Place in a preheated oven at 350°. Bake for about 20 to 30 minutes or until done. Remove from the oven, slice, and serve. Salmon will hold together better with the skin on; once the fish is baked, the skin is easier to remove.

Pork Chops with Cornbread Stuffing

6 1-inch-thick pork loin chops, split in the center
salt and black pepper to season

Cornbread Stuffing
½ cup oil or margarine
½ cup chopped onion
⅔ cup chopped celery
½ cup red bell pepper
1–1½ cups chicken broth
2 cups cooked cornbread pieces

Wash and damp dry the pork chops. Using a sharp knife, carefully split the outer round side of each pork chop to make a pocket that extends about halfway through the meat. Season each pork chop lightly inside and out with salt and pepper. Cover and set aside in the refrigerator while you make the stuffing.

In a skillet, over medium heat, add the onion, celery, and red bell pepper to the oil or margarine; sauté for 2 to 3 minutes, then add the chicken broth. Bring to a simmer and add the cornbread (the broth will be absorbed). Remove the pork chops from the refrigerator. Spoon stuffing from the skillet and stuff each pork chop; place the chops in a baking pan that has been greased or coated with cooking spray and is large enough for all the pork chops to fit without touching.

Put the pan in a preheated oven at 350° and bake until the pork chops and stuffing turn golden or lightly brown. Remove from the oven and serve your family a delight of bread and meat cooked together the way Momma used to fix it for us.

Grilling

As kids, when we played house, we would pretend to cook outside like Momma. We didn't see it as grilling; all we knew and loved at that time was to be little girls trying to cook like our parents because that was important.

And Pop and Momma didn't mind us playing house as long as we cleaned up after ourselves and did not get hurt.

We would go into the woods to gather piles of branches that we hauled back and placed between some old stacked bricks with an iron grill laid across. We gathered bricks for our outdoor stoves from the old torn-down fireplaces of an abandoned house. Sometimes we would build our grill under the mulberry tree and sometimes under the big oak tree where the pump was.

I've learned a great deal from cooking outside, trying to be like Momma. I remember the first big meal I cooked myself was some mud pies and several cans of boiled green leaves. Next it was the wild game or something from the house. I guess it was a part of growing up and not knowing it.

Some of the recipes that I am sharing here are as old as time, but I have come to love and enjoy them. I hope you will enjoy them your way.

Sizzling Grilled Shrimp

8–10 large or jumbo shrimp
1–2 teaspoons salt
1–2 teaspoons black pepper
1 teaspoon garlic powder
1 teaspoon paprika
¼ cup butter or margarine, melted

Peel and wash the shrimp. You can devein them if you like. Combine the salt, pepper, garlic powder, and paprika in a bowl or bag. Mix together well. Light the grill and line the rack with aluminum foil. When the grill is hot, brush one side of the shrimp with butter and sprinkle with the combined seasonings and place the shrimp on the heated foil about ½ inch apart. When the first side is grilled, brush on more butter and sprinkle with more seasonings and turn the shrimp. Remove the shrimp from the grill when they are done to your taste (I grill them for 2 to 3 minutes per side), and eat 'em up.

Grillin' Great Fish

2 6- to 8-ounce fish fillets of your choice
salt, black pepper, and garlic powder for seasoning
2 teaspoons butter or margarine, divided
½ medium-sized white or red onion, cut into strips
½ medium-sized red bell pepper, cut into strips
½ medium-sized green bell pepper, cut into strips

If you are using charcoal for grilling, give the grill time to cool down after lighting. Line the grill rack with aluminum foil. Wash and damp dry the fish. Sprinkle the fish lightly with salt, pepper, and garlic on both sides. Put 1 teaspoon of the margarine on the heated foil, place the fish on top of it, and let the fish cook. While the fish is cooking in one area of the grill, place the other teaspoon of margarine on the foil in another area and add the onion and bell peppers. Let the vegetables cook, turning them constantly. Turn the fish when the desired texture is achieved and let cook on the other side. When the vegetables are cooked, remove to a platter until the fish is done. When the fish is ready, place it on the platter, spread the vegetables on top of the grilled fish, and have a great fish dish.

Best Barbecue-Grill Honey Chicken

1 whole chicken, cut up
1 tablespoon salt
1 tablespoon black pepper
1 tablespoon garlic powder
1 tablespoon poultry seasoning
1 large onion, cut in ¼-inch rings
½–⅔ cup honey
1 cup barbecue sauce of your choice

Fire up the grill and let it burn off and cool down a little while you wash and damp dry the chicken parts. You may or may not wish to cover the rack with aluminum foil. In a bowl, mix together the salt, pepper, garlic powder, and poultry seasoning. Sprinkle the combined seasonings over the chicken. Refrigerate the seasoned chicken if the grill is not yet ready. When the grill is ready, place the chicken parts on the rack at least ¼ to ½ inch apart. Grill the onion rings at the same time—or as you remove the chicken if there is not enough room at first—until they are as soft as you like them. About 3 or 4 minutes before the chicken is done, pour the honey in a bowl and brush it on both sides of the chicken three or four times as the chicken continues to cook. When the chicken is done, serve it coated with your favorite barbecue sauce—or serve it up whatever way you like it.

Grilled Corn on the Cob in the Husk

6–8 ears of corn, husks on
½ cup butter, melted
2 tablespoons garlic powder or juice

Remove the top layer of the cornhusk, about 2 pieces. Combine the butter and garlic and brush all over the corn. Place the corn on a heated grill, turning occasionally as it cooks. Grill 3 to 5 minutes per side or until it's as done as you like.

Grilled Fresh Vegetables

Often we use canned or frozen vegetables because that's quick and easy, which is great when you're in a hurry. But if you like the taste of grilled food, grilling your vegetables is a real treat. Fresh grilled vegetables are healthy, tasty, and good for you. Try it; you might like it.

1 large zucchini, sliced
1 large yellow squash, sliced
1 large red bell pepper, sliced
1 large green bell pepper, sliced
1 large onion, cut into thick rings
½ teaspoon salt
½ teaspoon black pepper

In a medium bowl, combine the zucchini, yellow squash, bell peppers, and onion. Sprinkle the salt and pepper over the vegetables. Stir together and let sit in the refrigerator for about 15 to 20 minutes. Place the vegetables on a hot grill (coat the grill with cooking spray). Let vegetables cook for a few minutes on both sides, until they are as tender as you like. Remove and serve.

Seafood Isn't All Fried

As a child, I ate a lot of seafood caught fresh from the water that surrounds Daufuskie Island. At times we would eat shrimp, crabs, oysters, conch, and fish twice a day. Seafood was convenient for Momma and Pop, and they did not worry about the cost per pound or where they were going to get the freshest or biggest. The river and ocean had all that we needed, as fresh as it comes. We ate fish and seafood from the local waters year-round, and Momma would fix it up many different ways. All that was needed was some time and effort to collect it and bring it home.

I never knew, when I was little, that folks elsewhere didn't have the pleasure of getting seafood as we did. Whether it was seafood or not, we ate what was put on our plate or we went to bed hungry. Being choosy was not an option for us.

Many natives made a living by collecting and selling the island's different kinds of seafood. It was a way of life for those who didn't have a regular job to help support their family. Friends and family members who owned or worked on big shrimp boats from Savannah or Hilton Head would stop by our Daufuskie docks after being out on the water for days, dragging their nets to catch shrimp, fish, and crabs in Calibogue Sound and the Atlantic Ocean, which surround Daufuskie. Often the men who worked on the large shrimp boats would stop by to sell or give away their freshly caught seafood to help the natives.

When word got out that the shrimp boats would be stopping by, just about everyone gathered at the dock waiting to load up. Just like Pop and Momma, they would have their foot tubs, washtubs, buckets, and croaker sacks ready to be filled with shrimp, crabs, and fish. Everyone would load up and head home to have a great feast. Sometimes Momma and Pop or other islanders would invite the shrimpers to stay for a good home-cooked meal and a good drink of homemade wine. We girls knew that we had our work cut out for us cleaning the seafood when Momma and Pop returned home with bushel baskets of shrimp, crab, or fish. And we knew better than to complain or grumble even a little bit.

When Pop would go down to his favorite mullet hole and catch mullet by the sackful, he would share with families and neighbors around the island. Pop and Momma would try to give each household a fish per person.

When he got home, he would tell one of us girls to hand him a dish pan so that he could fill it up for Momma to cook enough for dinner. Most times we would have a portion of it left over for breakfast the next morning. Pop loved his mullet more than anything, and when he got home from sharing it with neighbors, he would holler at Momma, telling her not to take all evening cooking the fish because he was hungry. He would be soaked through from casting his mullet net and dragging it out of the water. Sometimes my sisters and I had to deliver the fish to elderly relatives and neighbors; other folks would come by for theirs.

Other times Pop would tell us girls to grab a pan and a knife and join him under the mulberry tree to clean the fish we were keeping. After a short while our noses would pick up the aroma of the good-smelling "smut-tered" fish Momma was making in the kitchen. Our stomachs would growl as we patiently waited to be called in to eat. When supper was ready, we would all sit at the table, say the blessing, and dig in.

If a lot of mullet were left over from Pop's big catch, Momma and Pop would prep the fish to be "corned," which was quite popular before we had refrigeration on the island, just as smoking meat was.

They would split the fish from the back of the head down to the tail end.

They would then heavily salt the mullet on both sides. Salt was used as a preservative to keep the fish from spoiling in hot weather with no refrigeration. A thick layer of regular cooking salt was used to dry the fresh fish and seal it. It was then strung on a piece of wire from the head and hung out to dry in the sun during the day. Before dark the fish was put in what we called a corner house or smokehouse. This process was repeated for several days or sometimes a week, until the fish was fully corned. When it came time to cook the smelly corned fish, Momma would unstring the ones she wanted and boil them several times in hot water to draw off the heavy layer of salt and tenderize the fish.

We were not fond of corned fish, but a meal was a meal. Even though we would turn our noses up at the unpleasant odor of the fish while it was being processed, corned fished was part of our diet. We had trust in Momma, and she knew how to turn something that didn't smell right to us into something tasty.

Preparing seafood was not fun: heading and peeling shrimp, boiling and picking bushels of crabs, scaling and cleaning tubfuls of fish, and cracking or shucking sackfuls of conch and oysters was plenty of work. But when we had fresh seafood, we didn't have to worry about where our next meal would come from.

Boiled, baked, or steamed food tastes great and is less fattening and much healthier than fried food. Boiling avoids the fat that frying adds to food, and boiling can be a great way to prepare seafood, like the wonderful bounty that we used to enjoy on 'Fuskie. Years ago, when Momma cooked a meal and fed us as we sat around the breakfast or dinner table with our plates piled high, we didn't give a second thought to what eating a lot of pork and fried food was doing to us. We always ate a stomachful without knowledge of it being bad, because most of the time we worked so hard before or after a meal we would burn off many of the calories that we ate.

Local Sea Island Country Boil

This is a Sea Island boil that everyone can enjoy. Making it was fun because we would catch the crabs, dig for the clams, cast for the shrimp, and grow the garlic, onion, celery, and corn. The few other ingredients, Momma would have bought during one of her monthly shopping trips and stored on the shelf in the kitchen.

We cooked this outside in a very large washtub or a barrel cut in half to accommodate the large amount of seafood. What a feast to gather around and eat a bellyful as you worked through the high pile of seafood and vegetables. We would have this feast during some of our big celebrations and gatherings. Getting together was about enjoying good company and the fresh seafood. Maybe you'd like to try it and get the pleasure of a great meal. Invite some good friends and have yourself a down yondah good time.

¼–⅓ cup Old Bay Seasoning or other seafood seasoning
4–6 large onions, cut into wedges
4–6 stalks of celery, cut in half or in thirds
8–10 cloves garlic
¼–⅓ cup crushed red pepper
6 bay leaves
2–3 pounds small clams
1 bushel blue crabs (optional)
5–8 pounds smoked sausage, cut into 3-inch pieces
15–20 small ears of corn, shucked
3–4 pounds potatoes (red or white), cut in half or in thirds
10–15 pounds medium to large shrimp

When cooking this amount, it would be best to do it outside over an open fire.

Fill a 5-gallon pot one-quarter to one-third full of water. Add the Old Bay seasoning to the pot and stir; add the onions, celery, garlic, crushed pepper, and bay leaves; stir. Taste test to get the flavor you want. Wash the clams, crabs, sausage, and corn. When the water in the large pot starts to boil, add the clams, crabs, sausage, and corn and cook for about 5 to 8 minutes. Next add the potatoes and boil for 5 more minutes. Then add the shrimp and let boil for 4 to 6 more minutes. Remove the meat, seafood, and vegetables from the water and place on a flat surface to cool for eating.

You can add other seafood to this boil or make up and add your own special seasoning. The more the better. Some folks like to add beer to the pot. Others like a few cans of beer to help them enjoy this feast, but that should be for adults only, please.

Gullah Garlic Butter Shrimp

You can cook this recipe spicy or mild.

2 sticks butter or margarine
¼ cup olive or vegetable oil
1 tablespoon salt
1 large onion, cut in thin wedges
2 cloves fresh garlic, crushed
juice of 1 lemon
5 pounds medium or large shrimp
6 ounces hot sauce (optional)

Put the butter, oil, salt, onion, garlic, and lemon juice in a large pot. Sauté over medium heat for 2 to 3 minutes, until the onion starts to turn clear. Add the shrimp and stir while cooking for 4 to 6 minutes. Do not leave unattended; the butter will burn. Once the shrimp turns pink enough for you, empty the contents of the pot into a large bowl. If you like it spicy, add the hot sauce and toss to coat the shrimp. Refrigerate or let cool for 30 to 60 minutes. Toss the shrimp a few times while cooling to season well. You can reheat this or eat it cold. Dig in and have yourself a good time.

Bushel Basket of Boiled Crabs

Boiling crabs was fun when we all gathered in the backyard. My sisters and I would share some of the chores, and we also had certain chores to do separately. No one got to sit around and watch the others work. Working together got the job done faster. We would gather piles of wood under the black washtub or cut-off barrel used for boiling crabs. Someone had to make sure the tub had enough water before adding the crabs and lighting the fire.

The crabs have to be placed in the water before it gets hot. If you put the crabs in hot water, they will go into shock and drop their claws immediately; if you put the crabs in cool water or water at room temperature, most of the claws will stay attached while boiling. A few claws will always detach, but most will stay on.

We would catch, boil, and pick lots of bushel baskets filled with crabs, sometimes two or three times a week during the warm spring and summer months. Even though the biggest job was picking the meat from the crabs after they were boiled, getting dozens of live crawling crabs from a bushel basket into a tub for boiling was not easy.

My sisters and I enjoyed watching Pop as he would put his bare hands into the bushel basket of snapping claws reaching up at his every move. Pop did not fear the snapping crabs; he would let us know that there was nothing to be afraid of, saying, "A little bite ain't dat bad." That was easy for him to say, but we didn't dare risk it. Getting bit by a crab hurts because crabs don't like to turn you loose when they grab on to you. We would sometimes witness Pop getting bit more than once by the crabs, but all he did was shake them off quickly and say, "Dat bugger got me."

TIP: Wear heavy gloves or use long-handled tongs to transfer snapping crabs from the basket to the water for boiling.

Occasionally a crab would crawl out of the tub and fall onto the sand, trying to run away. Watching with sharp eyes, we would get a stick and carefully place the crab on its back, holding it down so that Pop could it pick up by the two back fins. We were too afraid to pick up the crabs. Pop would rinse the sandy crab off with fresh water and then place it back into the pot to boil with the others.

Gradually the water began to heat. The crabs would scramble over each other trying to get out of the tub. Pop would sprinkle salt over them and cover them with a croaker sack or something solid enough to keep them in the pot. Sometimes the crabs would be left alone while boiling for a short period or watched by us girls as they changed color from dark blue green to pretty bright red on the backside and off-white on the belly. After the water starts to boil, the crabs cook in only about 5 to 8 minutes.

Islanders have another way, independent of the clock, of telling if the crabs are ready: turn a few crabs over on their backs and see if some of them (not all) have popped their belly button; if the belly button is open, this is a sign that the crab has boiled enough. Use caution as you remove the crabs from the hot water. Place the crabs on a flat surface to drain the excess water and to cool before you try to handle and pick them.

1 bushel crabs, rinsed under running water
¼–½ box of salt or seasoning salt

Fill a large pot one-quarter full with water. Bring the water to a boil and add the crabs; immediately add enough water (hot or cold) to cover the crabs. Follow Pop's instructions above, boiling for 5 to 8 minutes or until the belly buttons pop, and you, too, will enjoy the fun and work of boiling crabs.

Tangy Lemon Shrimp

Boiling shrimp is easy; you can do it without making a mess or spending much time.

Some folks like their shrimp cooked for only 3 minutes, but there are folks, like me, who have to have them cooked a little bit more. When cooking shrimp, the texture is up to you. Many folks can't eat shrimp because they are high in cholesterol, but for those of us that don't have a problem, let's eat up while bearing that fact in mind. And remember, the longer you boil shrimp, the tougher they get.

  1–2 pounds shrimp, heads on or off
  1½ quarts water
  1 tablespoon salt or choice of seasoning
  1 teaspoon black pepper
  3–4 tablespoons lemon juice
  1 medium-sized onion, cut in half (optional—use as much as you like)

Rinse the shrimp and let them drain. Put the water in a medium to large pot (it should be just enough to barely cover the shrimp); add the salt, pepper, lemon juice, and, if you like, onion; stir. Add the shrimp. Bring to a boil and let the shrimp cook for about 3 to 6 minutes; the shrimp will turn pink when done. Drain or remove shrimp from cooking water. Place the shrimp in a pan or on a flat surface to cool. Peel, eat, and enjoy!

Boiled Conch

Whether you call it conch or whelk, it is a tasty seafood that sometimes has to be cooked for hours so that you can chew it without losing a few teeth. The larger the conch, the tougher it is and the longer it takes for it to become tender. If you are a conch lover, the wait is worth it; a love of conch is, however, an acquired taste. When conch is cooked right and seasoned properly, it can be very tasty.

The first step is to get the conch out of the shell. One way to do this is to smash the hard shell with an ax or hammer to crack it open. Another is to boil the conch and pull it out of the shell with a fork. Prepared this way, it can be used in a stew or fried in a fritter.

  8–10 medium to large conch, in their shells
  water
  1 tablespoon salt

Wash the conch with a water hose or in a bucket of water to remove mud and sand. Place the conch in a large pot and add water to barely cover them. Add the salt and bring to a boil. Boil for about 30 to 45 minutes. Please take caution when removing the conch from the water: the conch shell is very hot and will remain that way for a while after it has been removed from the hot water. Use a safety mitten or glove or a slotted spoon to remove the conch.

Once the conch has cooled enough to handle, stick a sturdy fork into the meaty part of the conch under the oval shell on top. Angle the fork upward and, holding firmly, pull outward. The meat of the conch will come out of the shell, along with the fat and other part of the conch that is buried deep in the shell. Even though you can eat the conch meat, it will be somewhat chewy at this time. Many like to eat the conch raw; others like to tenderize it before eating it.

Steamed or Roasted Oysters

Oysters are special; they produce one of nature's most precious jewels, the pearl. It does not grow in all oysters, but every chance you get to open an oyster, you hope that there's a pearl inside for you. Oysters are also said to be an aphrodisiac.

On Daufuskie they grow on the banks of the marsh along the water in small to large clusters. Some people love to eat the slimy oysters just as they are shucked from the shell; others prefer them cooked. Oysters can be difficult to open, and their top shells have a razor-sharp edge; you can get a very nasty, deep cut if you do not handle them with care. It is a good idea to wear protective gloves while opening them.

Picking (collecting) and shucking oysters goes back centuries. It was and still is a way of life for some folks. Pop and Momma would tell us children stories of how Daufuskie had one of the most productive oyster factories "back in the day." Many people remember the island ladies and men getting up as early as the sun and heading off to the riverfront to spend the whole day picking and shucking oysters, day after day. Momma says she remembers how the men did the collecting (picking) of oysters in bateau boats while the women stayed at the factory and shucked oysters from sunup to sundown. Gallons and gallons of oysters were hand shucked and packed by native islanders and shipped off to other places. Momma said my grandmother and great-grandmother could shuck oysters really fast.

Shortly before I arrived in the world, the oyster factory was closed. The building was still there when I was a girl, and we kids used to play in it before it was torn down. I am glad I got a chance at least to touch a part of the island's history that once was.

20 pounds (or more) oysters, singles and clusters
    (20 pounds will feed 4–6 people, although some
    oyster lovers can eat the entire amount)

Gather a big stack of wood for building a fire. (This is great on the beach, or somewhere else where you can build a fire safely, and is fun to do with a group of family and friends.)

Steamed Oysters

On each side of the stacked wood, place some cement blocks or bricks stacked somewhat higher than the wood. Light the fire and place a sturdy piece of tin over the fire, with either end resting securely on the stacked blocks. Spread the oysters out on the tin; be careful because the tin gets hot quickly. Place a croaker sack (burlap sack) in some water to soak, then place the wet burlap sack, dripping with water, on top of the oysters on the heated tin. The heat from the tin over the fire combined with the wet burlap sack steams the oysters open. When they have opened and it is time to remove the burlap sack, use caution. Use a shovel to move the hot oysters from the tin onto a flat surface to cool.

Everyone waits with a knife to open the shells, remove the plump oysters, and enjoy. When using an oyster knife or a butter knife to open an oyster, place the knife where the oyster has opened from the steam, push the knife into the oyster, and pry open the top shell. Then take your knife, cut loose the attached oyster, and slurp it up. Many people wear a glove on the hand that holds the oyster to avoid getting nicked with the oyster knife.

Roasted Oysters

You don't necessarily need a piece of tin if you want to roast the oysters: they cab be shoveled directly into the fire. When you place them in the fire, step away and don't stand too close to the fire. When the oyster shells start to heat, they can break off or pop away, flying into the air. These flying pieces of sharp, hot shell could be very dangerous. Use a shovel to remove the oysters carefully from the fire when they begin to open, allow to cool, and then open in the same way described for steamed oysters. When the oyster is roasted, it has a really good, smoky flavor, and is cooked dry, without the slippery liquid of raw or steamed oysters.

Desserts and Cookies

Whether we thought of it as the beginning of the week or the last day of the week, Sunday was the Lord's Day. All the major work was done throughout the week and ended on Saturday. Certain chores, like feeding the animals, were done every day, but work on Sundays was limited. Sunday was the time for eating a much bigger dinner and getting together with family and friends.

Early in the week, Momma would begin planning for Sunday dinner, checking her cupboards and rice can, making sure that she had enough of everything so she could fix her big Sunday breakfast and dinner. We kids couldn't wait to sit down and enjoy every bite of what Momma had cooked for Sunday's big feast. Like many island natives, Momma always prepared big meals during the week, but Sunday dinner had to be bigger and better. Sometimes certain meats or vegetables were put aside just for Sunday.

The meals were always planned with the expectation that guests might be dropping in. Sunday was more than just a day for church and rest; it was also a time to visit the sick and shut-ins or to invite friends and family over to break bread and drink homemade wine. Momma liked nothing more than to have folks over to eat her cooking.

After dinner was over, Pop would break out the homemade wine as the adults went outdoors to sit on the porch or under the shade tree in the backyard if the weather was nice. They did this so that we kids didn't get an earful of some things we didn't need to hear. If it was winter, they would all gather around the big dining room table near the wood heater. We kids had to clean up and finish our few chores before dark. That would keep us out of their company if we could not leave the house. We could hear the laughter getting louder as they told old jokes and stories and drank more wine.

It seemed as if Momma never tired of being creative in the kitchen, cooking all day long sometimes on the hot wood-burning stove. I guess I have inherited that love for cooking, as my mother inherited it from her mother, and as have all the good cooks in my family who know how to "throw down a meal" or "put da' foot in it" as some natives would say.

The native ladies of Daufuskie Island have always cooked and shared their meals with others. Most folks didn't mind if someone stopped by for a visit and got a good home cooked meal at the same time. Grandmomma Blossom loved to cook big meals all through the week, even when she and Granddaddy Josephus were the only ones eating. Grandmomma believed that some kind of food should always be cooking in case a hungry soul dropped in. And when people dropped in and said yes out of respect to her offer of food, she would pile their plates high, guide them to the table, and say "Sit down ya, and eat all dat food on yo' plate; dare is plenty mo' in da pot." Grandmomma, like most folks on the island, didn't believe anyone should go around hungry.

One of my favorite Sunday meals was—and still is—red rice or crab rice, collard greens, fried chicken or fried ribs, macaroni and cheese, shrimp and tada salad, and one or two of Momma's surprise desserts. Eating everything on our plate was a must or we could not have any dessert or drink our Kool-Aid. Momma had a long list of desserts, including bread pudding, sweet potato pie, sweet potato bread, lemon meringue pie, apple pie, pear bread, blackberry dumpling, peach cobbler, potato bread, banana pudding or some hand-churned homemade ice cream with fresh fruit. I could go on and on.

Cornbread, biscuits, and cracklin' bread were mostly served during the week, while sweets were served mostly on Sunday. We got to eat sweet bread on the weekdays only if Momma felt like baking something. Her tasty cornbread or fluffy biscuits smothered with pure cane syrup was the only sweet bread we were going to get before Sunday.

Many things mattered, but two things that didn't matter to us were

NIGHT

115

whether our tableware was matching and whether it looked good. Our nonmatching silverware, plates, and glasses (which were jelly and peanut butter jars) were cared for as if they were china. We sat in old odd, run-down chairs. Dinnertime was not about what we sat on or ate from but the love that went into preparing the meal. Material things did not change or make our ways or who we were. We were happier when we didn't know why certain material things were considered better than others.

Country Candied Yams with Raisins

These days we have several kinds of sweet potatoes, but as a child I knew only one kind. Really sweet and juicy when it was cooked, this potato had dark red skin and was deep orange-red inside. Whether it was baked, boiled, or roasted, it was always sweet.

When the weather was cool and we worked most of the day outside in the yard or the woods, Momma and Pop would let us build a fire in the backyard. Once the fire got good and hot, we put sweet potatoes under the hot coals. The potatoes would cook fast in the hot coals, the outer skins burning and the sweet juicy syrup bubbling out. We would watch them carefully once the syrup began to ooze, knowing that it was not going to be long before we could enjoy them.

We used a stick to keep the hot coals on top of the potatoes, being careful when digging them out. This was a lot of fun for my sisters and me, especially if a family member or friend joined us. These were happy moments, cooking outside with our parents' permission. We would squat around the fire, eating the tasty, hot, roasted sweet potatoes. Momma knew how much we loved sweet potatoes, and she would make us sweet desserts like this one and the one in the next recipe.

6–8 medium-sized sweet potatoes or yams, peeled and sliced
½ cup whole milk, warmed
1 teaspoon vanilla extract
1 cup pineapple juice

⅔ cup sugar

⅓ stick butter, softened

⅔ teaspoon ground cinnamon

½ teaspoon ground allspice

⅔ cup raisins

½ lemon, thinly sliced

Put the sweet potatoes in a medium bowl and set aside. In a bowl, mix together the milk, vanilla extract, pineapple juice, and sugar. Pour this liquid mixture over the sweet potatoes. Add the butter, cinnamon, allspice, and raisins and stir to combine. Transfer to a baking pan and smooth out the top. Place the lemon slices over the sweet potato mixture. Bake in a preheated 375° oven for about 45 to 60 minutes. Remove from the oven and enjoy hot or cold.

Southern Sweet Tada Pie with Pecan Topping

6–8 medium to large sweet potatoes

1½ sticks butter

1¼ cups sugar

5 large eggs

2½ tablespoons self-rising flour

½ cup whole milk

½ cup condensed milk

1 teaspoon grated lemon rind

¾ teaspoon ground cinnamon

¼ teaspoon ground allspice

¼ teaspoon ground or fresh grated nutmeg

9-inch pastry pie crust, uncooked

½ cup pecan halves

Boil the sweet potatoes, left whole, in a pot of water until soft enough to be easily pierced with a fork. Pour off the water and let the potatoes cool. Peel the potatoes and place them in a large bowl. Mash or whip until smooth; add the butter, sugar, eggs, and flour, and mix together. Add the whole and condensed milk, lemon rind, cinnamon, allspice, and nutmeg. Mix together well, then pour the mixture into the pie crust. Neatly arrange the pecan halves to cover the top of the pie. Bake in a preheated oven at 350° for about 45 minutes, or until the pie crust is slightly brown. Remove from the oven and let cool.

Peanut Butter Cookies

Makes 1½–2 dozen.

If you know about cookies, then you know that there's nothing like the taste of a good old-fashioned peanut butter cookie dunked in a glass of cold milk. Momma didn't make many cookies for us during my younger years; she was always too busy mixing and fixing everything else.

But I remember having the best fresh-baked peanut butter cookies with lunch at school. My school had several very good cooks while I was there, but one cook in particular made the best-tasting peanut butter cookies. She knew that they were one of our favorites, and she would prepare a batch at least once a week for us to enjoy. She knew how much we loved them from the smiles on our faces, and we kept coming back for more.

The peanut butter that she used in her cookies came in large tin cans, and it was not very soft, so she had to spend a lot of time to get the right texture for the cookies.

Friday was usually cookie day, and we loved smelling the aroma of the peanut butter cookies baking in the oven in the school kitchen. Our school was small, with only two classrooms, two bathrooms, a short hallway, and a kitchen and lunchroom. It was sometimes hard for us to keep still in our chairs and concentrate on our lessons as the smell of cookies and other good food flowed down the hall into our classrooms. We would watch the big clock on the wall over our teacher's head and count down the minutes until lunchtime. If it seemed to be taking too long, we would take turns asking to be excused just so we could get a better smell or take a look in the kitchen.

After lunch we could go outside to play our favorite games. Sometimes a few of us girls would volunteer to help wash the dishes and clean up the kitchen instead. We didn't mind wiping down the lunchroom tables, sweeping the floors, and putting away the dishes while the other kids went outside for recess. We knew that we would be rewarded with the leftover peanut butter cookies or with extra helpings the next day for giving a hand. And sometimes that was better than going outside to play. Our cook appreciated our helping hands.

¼ cup shortening, softened
¼ cup butter or margarine, softened
¾ cup crunchy peanut butter
½ cup granulated sugar
½ cup brown sugar, packed
1 large egg
1¼ cups all-purpose flour
¾ teaspoon baking soda
½ teaspoon baking powder
½ teaspoon salt

Preheat oven to 375°. In a medium-sized bowl, mix together the shortening, butter, peanut butter, granulated and brown sugar, and egg. Blend in the flour, baking soda, baking powder, and salt. Place in the refrigerator and let chill for about 15 to 20 minutes. Shape the dough into 1-inch balls and place them about 3 inches apart on a lightly greased cookie sheet. Use a fork to gently flatten and shape the cookies. Bake for 10 to 12 minutes until slightly brown, or a little longer if you prefer them crispier.

Chocolate Chip Cookies with Pecans

Makes about 2½ dozen.

⅔ cup shortening, softened
⅔ cup butter or margarine, softened
1 cup granulated sugar
1 cup brown sugar, packed
2 large eggs
2 teaspoons vanilla extract
3¼ cups all-purpose flour
1 teaspoon baking soda
1 teaspoon salt
1 cup pecan halves
12 ounces semisweet chocolate chips

Preheat oven to 375°. In a bowl, mix together the shortening, butter, granulated and brown sugar, eggs, and vanilla extract. Add the flour, baking soda, salt, pecans, and chocolate chips and combine. Scoop up the dough and place by the rounded spoonful, about 1 inch apart, on lightly greased cookie sheets. Bake for 8 to 10 minutes, or until done.

Oatmeal Raisin Cookies

Makes about 2½ dozen.

1 cup shortening, softened
2 cups granulated sugar
2 large eggs
2½ cups uncooked oats
3¼ cups all-purpose flour
2 teaspoons baking soda

1 teaspoon salt
1 cup whole milk or buttermilk
1½ cups raisins

Preheat oven to 350°. In a large bowl, mix the shortening and sugar together until creamy. Add the eggs one at a time, mixing well after each addition. Combine until the mixture is fluffy. Combine the oats, flour, baking soda, and salt in a separate bowl. Beat in the dry ingredients, alternating with buttermilk, about a third at a time. Add the raisins and stir to combine. Scoop the dough up by the rounded spoonful and place ¼ inch apart on lightly greased cookie sheets. Bake for 12 to 15 minutes. Remove from the oven and let cool.

Pecan Crunch Cookies

Makes about 2½ dozen.

2 sticks butter
1½ cups 10x confectioners' sugar
1 large egg
½ teaspoon baking soda mixed in 1 tablespoon hot water
2½ cups all-purpose flour
1 cup pecan pieces

Preheat oven to 350°. In a bowl, cream the butter and sugar together. Add the egg and beat well. Add the hot water and baking soda mixture. Add the flour a little at a time. Stir in the pecan pieces. Roll the dough out to about ¼ inch thick on a flat, floured surface. Use a cookie cutter or a jelly jar or water glass to cut the dough. Re-form the scraps and cut again until all the dough is used. Place ¼ inch apart on lightly greased cookie sheets. Bake for about 8 to 10 minutes. Remove and let cool. Enjoy 'em.

Gullah Folk Beliefs & Home Remedies

Living with Nature

I remember the days when folks like Pop, Momma, and other Sea Island natives had their own ways. It was the only know-how that island folks had back then. Native islanders believed some crazy stuff. It wasn't as if they taught us children all of these things, but they didn't make them secrets either. We just picked up on them as a part of daily living. We would learn about many things during storytelling time around the fireplace or in hearing the older folks talk among themselves.

Many people talk about or treasure facts and fictions of the past, but there is something different about experiencing those facts and fictions firsthand, having lived with them. Folks from the mainland would shake their heads and say to themselves, "Those island folks are crazy." But no matter what others thought, we had our own way of life. Other folks thought that we were strange because we held onto the beliefs of our ancestors. But, like my granddaddy used to say, "A heap may see, but only a few knows."

Living on Daufuskie had a certain charm and peace. We knew we would always have clothes on our backs, plenty of food on the table, and a roof over our heads; we lived one day at a time. We made it work because we accepted nature and all that it had to give us.

And part of accepting nature was learning to respect it, including the storms that blew across the island. I never heard of lightning striking anyone during my time on Daufuskie, mainly because everyone had the utmost respect for it and took necessary precautions.

Momma said electricity came to the island in the early 1950s, but it wasn't until the late '60s that we got electrical wires run to the old wooden house where we were living. Even so, Momma always kept her oil lamps in a safe place in a corner, ready for emergency outages. At times, bad storms would cause the power to go out, and sometimes it could take days or even weeks for a broken electric line to be repaired.

Those times living on Daufuskie without a television or radio to inform us about the weather made us wiser as we learned nature's ways. We learned how to read the clouds before a thunderstorm and how to rely on signs from nature telling us about the weather and what would be happening: the high and low tides, the sun and the moon, even the behavior of animals. We learned to live by these signs in nature.

We would take notice of the ways the animals behaved when a bad storm was brewing. They had their own signs. The chickens would start cackling and seeking shelter close to each other; the cows' mooing turned as the thunder roared; the dogs barked constantly, peeking out from under the house; the pigs would oink and squeal for long periods, staying close together. All would hurry and head for shelter as the heavy clouds formed and blocked the sun, the fast-moving pillows of clouds racing across the sky.

Pop would say that he could smell the rain coming before it started. He would point to the sky, showing us the different kinds of clouds and tell us what was going to happen. He would look up in the sky, watching a few clouds start. Then they would change, gathering fast. Sometimes he would say, "That weather is headed our way. Y'all churn know what ya gotta get done, so get a move on. Or do I need to give ya sumptin ta help ya?"

As kids, we tried to get in some playtime as we hurried to finish all our chores before the big downpour. We liked to play in the raindrops while we finished up our work if it was not coming down too hard. If Pop felt it was going to hit us hard and last a while, we had extra chores.

More wood had to be chopped and brought in from the woodpile; that was way out in the backyard under the old oak tree during the summer and under the mulberry tree near the house during the cooler winter months. My sisters and I would race one another as the sharp lightning struck and the loud thunder roared; we would duck when this happened as we strained to carry oversized armloads of chopped wood to stack behind the woodstove in the kitchen and to fill extra boxes stacked high on the back porch in a corner.

Before a storm, water had to be pumped by the bucketfuls, carried inside, and covered with a lid or a clean towel. But during a storm, Momma liked to catch some of the rainwater pouring from the rooftop so that we could have plenty of extra water. Momma was happy to know that it was going to rain to help her garden, but the rainwater was collected for other uses too. She would place a washtub at the corner of the house and some foot tubs on the sides, where the rain would pour off the rooftop during the bad weather. This meant less pumping and hauling of water for us.

Pop and Momma both believed that the rainwater we caught for use around the house was the purest and best-tasting water of all. Washing our hair with it made it grow longer, cooking with it kept us safe and healthy, and bathing our bodies with it made us cleaner and blessed all over. Pop would often remind us, "Dat's God's watah from up dere and dere's none bettah," and Momma would agree with a smile. We would sometimes catch the rainwater for the animals to drink so that they would all get blessed, too.

During lightning and thunder storms, we had to make sure that all our animals were protected. Our work and milk cows had to be brought in from the old field where they grazed, sometimes way down the road from the house. They were then tied near the house for safety. They could not be left in the open field because they might seek shelter under the nearby pine trees, which tended to draw lightning. The chickens would all gather closer in the coop, and we would lock them in so that the lightning and thunder would not scare them off into the woods. The hogs, cats, and dogs were on their own, hiding under the house until it was all over.

Sometimes we would get the outside work done just in time before the downpour would make us run for cover. After the chores were completed and the animals were taken care of, we would get ready for the storm inside the house. Momma would help us gather all the lamps and put them on the big dining room table. We had to fill them with kerosene that was bought from the mainland; the lampshades had to be washed and dried before it got too dark inside the house. One after the other, the lamps were lit and placed in a safe place in each room, on a table or dresser, with the light turned down very low. This way we could see if we had to finish doing something, and our parents thought it was safer to have a little light in case we had to move around.

The rain would start to pour, beating hard against the tin rooftop, sounding like music to our ears and sometimes putting us to sleep; shortly after the downpour, some of the rain would begin to leak into the house through the holes in the roof. Momma would have us quickly place buckets, basins, pots, and pans around the house to catch the water.

During bad weather Pop and Momma made sure that we had gathered everything we would need because we weren't allowed outside or—except for necessary activities like placing pans to catch drips—allowed to move around the house, not even to look outside, until it was all over.

When a big storm was brewing, the loud thunder and lightning warned us to get ready; it was as if we were going to have a spell cast on us. At times like this, the lightning and thunder would be so loud that it felt as if it stroked the house the way it made the whole house tremble. When there was lots of lightning and thunder (Pop and Momma called thunder "loud claps"), Momma would help us hang white sheets over the front door, which was one-third glass, and any big mirrors in the house. This was done to protect the house from lightning entering, and it helped us feel safer.

We had to sit the storm out in a corner in the dark on the floor, trying to be quiet. Being in the dark was fun as we tried to play tag or hide and seek (our own version), hoping Pop and Momma wouldn't catch us, but they always did. Pop would say, "Stop dat playing. Y'all churn year me? God's talkin'. He wants ya ta listen."

A lot of superstitions were associated with storms. Many islanders believed that if it rained shortly after someone was buried, that meant his footprints were being washed away from the earth. And if it was raining and the sun was shining at the same time, that meant the devil was beating his wife and she was crying. The kitchen was off limits for any kind of cooking because a stove with fire in it has heat that draws lightning to it. Pop would say, "If dem lightning hit da stove and ya in dere, it'll knock ya ta da floor." We didn't want to find out if this was so.

Pop and Momma believed all these things and more because they had been taught to believe them by their parents and grandparents or because these things had happened to them or to someone they knew. Changing their minds and their ways was not possible. Their elders' words were the gospel truth. For centuries, these beliefs and superstitions had been passed down from one generation to another, and they believed what they were teaching us to be true. It was the way we had to survive on our Island named Daufuskie.

Sea Island Folk Beliefs

Some of the other things Pop and Momma taught us kids seem crazy now. If you broke a mirror, even by accident, you would have seven years of bad luck. We didn't have lots of mirrors, so when one was available, it seemed as if my two younger sisters and I always wanted to use it at the same time. However, we believed that two or more people should not look in the same mirror at the same time because the youngest would die first. (Ha! This helped keep them off my back since I'm the oldest.) Of course, that may have just been a way to say, "Don't be looking over my shoulder; find your own mirror."

We had many more beliefs about bad luck. Cats are great pets, and at times we had a few with various color patterns. Neither Pop nor Momma liked having a solid black cat at home, because if a black cat crossed in front of you going toward your left while walking down a road or path, you were going to have some bad luck follow you that day. And when something bad happened or you got a beating that day, you knew that the cause was that black cat crossing in front of you. You would also have bad luck if you walked backward, so even though it could be fun, we didn't often do it.

You know how sometimes when you comb your hair there seems to be more hair in the comb or brush than on your head? We believed you shouldn't throw your hair away; you should bury it in a hole near the house right after you finish combing your hair. If you threw it away or lost it and a bird made a nest with it, then you would go crazy.

We also had beliefs about good luck, but fewer than we had about misfortunes. If you were walking down a path or a road, and you found a coin heads up, you would pick it up and throw it over your right shoulder; this would give you good luck. If it was tails, you would leave it there unless you wanted more bad luck. Having a horseshoe over your front door or over all the doors in your house brought your family good luck and kept bad spirits away. If you stubbed your left foot, you stopped and turned around to the right in a full circle one time for good luck, even if it really hurt; you would do the opposite for the right foot.

Voodoo/Hoodoo

A lot of our superstitions and beliefs had to do with death and the spirit world. They were related to religious practices and beliefs originating in Africa and widespread in the Caribbean known collectively as voodoo or hoodoo. At one time, if the husband in a couple died first, the wife had to wear totally black clothing every day for six months. This didn't apply to the husband when the wife died first, and no one ever asked why.

Many folks wouldn't let their picture be taken, and some will not to this day. They believed that the camera would steal their soul. If you were alone and thought you heard someone calling your name, you would look around to see if anyone was there before you answered. We believed that if you answered and didn't see anyone, you could be answering to a ghost.

If we were asleep and dreamed that someone we once knew who was dead appeared and asked us to give him or her something, we were not supposed to do it. Folks believed that responding to the request would be giving someone over to death because the dead person wanted someone to join him or her.

When an elderly family member died, if the youngest family member living in the house was a "hand baby," that infant was always passed over the coffin during the burial. This was to keep the spirit of the deceased person from haunting or visiting the youngest child while he or she slept. It was said that when a child yelled out while sleeping and would not stop crying, a deceased person was visiting. Many folks believed that cursing would make a visiting spirit go away. We also believed that children are more able to see spirits (ghosts) than older people.

I can recall times when Momma used to hear strange noises although there was no one in the house except her. She would speak out, telling the spirit to go away: "I ain't got nothing for ya here." Nevertheless, we were taught to believe that the dead could not hurt you; only the living could do that.

'Fuskie Old-Fashioned Home Remedies

Home Remedies were, and to a degree still are, used by some folks in the Sea Islands. It was the only way that we knew how to help our ailing bodies. Island folks have depended on home remedies—the knowledge of nature's pure and simple ways—for generations as far back as anyone can remember. Island folks ate well and did the things that they knew. Like everyone else, we had to deal with variations in the climate and changes in our bodies, young or old.

Sickness will always be part of life's package of discomfort. We are only human, and there are some things we cannot control. We lived by the laws of nature that ruled the land, the ocean, and the air we breathed. If we were good to nature, it would be good to us.

Our toughest times were the winter months when the northeast wind would blow hard our way. More had to be done for us to stay safe and healthy, and together we did it. Sometimes the tin on the roof would nearly fly away in the strong, cold wind. Even though it was old, ugly, and beat-up, the tin rooftop used to look beautiful with icicles draped from it. On a chilly night, Pop and Momma would have us pull out our old reliable wood heater from the back porch where it had spent the long hot summer.

The wind whistled as it blew around the house, making it tremble, but we didn't fear. We had everything on hand because Momma always prepared herself. As the weather got cooler, she would start pulling her hand-made quilts out of the trunks where they were stored and putting them on the beds. She spent hours sewing these heavy quilts by hand during the summer months when she got a break from other housework.

These quilts were beautifully made from old clothes that were no longer wearable. We would help rip the old clothing apart and remove the loose threads. Clothes were made stronger then and lasted a lot longer. A dress could make its way through all the females in the family before it was used for quilt patches. When one of Momma's dresses got torn or became too small for her, she would make a smaller-sized dress for one of us. Material was never taken for granted; everything was used and it was stretched to the limit. All this and more was done by her busy hands; we had no sewing machine. And those padded quilts kept us warm all through the long, cold nights when we would snuggle together to warm up.

The wind would blow so hard entering the house that the kerosene lamp would flicker and almost go out. Pop wasn't one to "catch fire" in the wood heater until our first good chill, no matter what. "Put more clothes on" was his advice. But when that cold wind began to blow, he would tell us, "Catch dat fire ta da knock chill out." Then, when we were old enough, we had to get up first to catch a fire in the woodstove and wood heater.

Gathering around the comfort of the first fire in the wood heater meant winter had arrived. Both the wood heater and woodstove helped warm the old, falling-down house. Momma would tell us girls to open up all the doors to the rooms to let the heat warm up each room. By the time we went to bed, our bedroom would be warm enough. Sitting up too late meant burning more wood, and that meant the need to chop fire logs and bring them in. Early to bed meant early to rise in our house so that more could get done during the course of the day.

The houses on the island were built without insulation, and the thin tin roofs had holes. At night, the shutters would be closed tight and everyone accounted for because, no matter what was wrong with what we had, we were happy to be warm inside together after a hard day's work. We would come together at the table for supper or gather around the wood heater to listen to stories; we felt as if the world beyond us couldn't get any better than what we had right there.

As the seasons changed, so did our bodies, and being country smart went a long way in helping us deal with the changes. Momma was the best doctor, who really knew her stuff well; she often told us how she learned the different ways of the plants and herbs that once grew plentifully on the island. She learned from her parents and from Grandmomma, who had learned from their parents and grandparents. Remedies have been passed down through the generations for as long as my family and others have been on the Sea Islands.

Remedies were second nature to Momma, and she knew a lot about nature and its cures. When in need, she would go into the woods to pop, break, or dig up what she knew was best for our ailments. She would mix up the things she collected and make a cure that got us going again. And one thing was certain: Momma knew where to go to find the right shrubs, leaves, bark, and roots. Most times what she needed grew right in our back-yard or not too much farther away.

Momma knew the right herb to pick just like she knew exactly which holly to pick. "Don't ya pick da holly wit da red berries," she would warn us; "da are not good for you." She sought out leaves with just the right shape before picking them; she would describe which roots were the best; and she knew how to look at the bark on trees to distinguish one from an-other when they had no leaves in winter.

The woods on Daufuskie are slowly being cleared, and the land on both ends of the island is now being developed, with big houses spring-ing up. Many of the herbs and roots that we knew and used are slowly disappearing, and the native knowledge of their use is disappearing with them. Younger folks are not as interested as those before them had been. We can no longer find some of Momma's regulars, like sampson snakeroot and black root; even the "like Pulaski" (life everlasting—commonly called "rabbit tobacco") is harder to find now. So is the toothache tree whose bark helped get us through some tough tooth pain during long nights with nowhere to go for help.

When we were growing up, Momma did all she could to make sure that we stayed well. She kept us padded down with two or three layers of clothes from head to toe in the cold weather, and she would check us over before we left the house, even just to go play or work in the yard. I recall how she made us extra underslips out of the flowery cotton sacks used to hold 50 pounds of rice or flour.

Daufuskie did not have a doctor sitting around waiting for patients to walk through the door. Nor was there a walk-in clinic on a streetcorner to patch up a minor cut or bruise. To get to the doctors on the mainland re-quired a boat ride and lots of organizing. Momma knew that distance and time were not always on our side. Going over to the mainland was much more than just taking a boat ride; you had to get in touch with someone who was available to meet you at the dock with a car and take you where you needed to go. Sometimes this could turn into an all-day trip away from work or home.

At the beginning of the school year, a nurse and a doctor would come over from the town of Bluffton on the mainland to make sure that all of us children had received our vaccinations. How we hated to see those folks coming in their white uniforms; but our parents were glad. They knew that, along with our home remedies, the medicines that the doctor and nurse gave us would help keep us well, and they were free. I remember when the doctor and nurse from across the way gave us a lump of sugar with a drop or two of some pink stuff on it for polio. That tasted OK, and I liked it because it was sweet.

Like all mothers everywhere, Momma just wanted to make her kids' pain or sniffles go away. When a big hug or kiss wasn't enough, she would use the remedies that she believed in.

Momma was our doctor around the clock. We relied on her to make every ache and pain go away. A sniffle, a cough, or a little sneeze meant it was time to get fixed. If a batch of one of her remedies wasn't already waiting, she would gather a bucket and/or a croaker sack along with a hoe and a sharp knife, and head out the back door. Off into the woods she would go, sometimes with us at her side, returning later with all she needed.

We thought we could outsmart our parents, but we didn't get away with it any more than most kids do. We were warned that they had invented the tricks we were trying to play on them. I found out at an early age that playing sick in order to stay home from school was not a good thing. The minute everyone else had gone to school and you thought you were feeling better so you could get up and play, you were in for a treat. There was always work around the house that needed to be done. If you felt well enough to play, you were well enough to work until the others returned. Once was enough for me; I never tried that again.

Caution!

Home remedies, like any medicines, are not to be used for fun or as jokes. Never take a home remedy if you are not sure what it can do for or to you.

Knowledge is always the key, so learn about any remedy and be aware of the good and bad sides of it. Even though home remedies can be helpful, they can also bring you great harm if misapplied. There are hundreds of look-alike plants, roots, and berries out there. Don't assume you know.

Educate yourself and learn more about home remedies and the ingredients that go into them before you take a chance on causing yourself harm. And remember that what someone else suggests works for him or her might not be what is best for you. Our bodies do not all respond in the same way.

Here is a selection of home remedies that we used to help our ailing bodies feel better. Momma usually knew what to do for us, though she had to take a chance at times. These are the old ways we used on 'Fuskie. Under no circumstances should these remedies be thought of as a substitute for proper medical attention in the case of a serious condition or complaint. Sometimes we didn't have any other way, but because Momma learned from those that taught her how to do it the right way, we survived.

Ear Cleaning: Flicking the Right Kind of Feather

When Momma and Pop felt that they were getting a little hard of hearing and their ears needed cleaning, they would send one of us children out to the chicken yard to gather a handful of feathers from a pullet (a female chicken). They examined closely the feathers we brought them and carefully selected the right one for the job. They would never use a rooster feather to clean their ears: it is said that cleaning your ears with a rooster feather will make you crazy. A hen feather was all they used.

Cold Symptoms: Sniffles, Coughing, Fever, Sneezing

Once the cold season began, Momma would enter the woods and bring back whatever she felt she needed, because she wanted to have on hand a fixin' for whatever was about to ail us. She would use this fixin' in addition to her hot toddy described in the preceding chapter (page ooo). One of her best cold remedies was a mixture of wild holly bush (it had to be the right one, the kind that grows wild on the island and doesn't produce berries), pine tops, life everlasting, and lemon.

"Come ya, Sallie Ann," Momma would call. So I would collect the ax, hoe, and croaker sack for our hunt to gather the fixings for her cold remedies. She would show me how to break off certain pieces of pine and holly branches, and she would remind me how to tell the difference between the right one and the wrong one.

Once we found the right ones, we had to shake them to get rid of bugs.

Then we would take home all that we had gathered and run cold water over them to wash them. Momma would have us strip the pine needles and holly leaves off the branches; then we would put the needles and leaves in a pot to boil, adding 4 to 6 pieces of the life everlasting herb. Momma would take the rest of the life everlasting, tie it in bundles, and hang it in a corner on the back porch to dry. She would leave it hanging there until she needed it.

After the concoction boiled for about half an hour, it would simmer on the stove on medium heat all during cold season. Momma would add a whole or half lemon before it was time to drink it to help take away some of the bitter taste. Maybe Momma believed that the lemon helped, but we always thought it was bitter and nasty, too. Nevertheless, our bodies got rid of what was trying to start and stopped what was trying to get in. We didn't have any of the good-tasting grape- or cherry-flavored stuff.

When a pot wasn't already on the woodstove brewing with some of Momma's shrubs and roots, and something had to be done in a hurry, Momma would always have a backup in the pantry. She would pull out a bottle of Three Sixes (666's), castor oil, or cod liver oil, or she would take out the ingredients to mix up the following cold remedy. Pop would be standing by with his belt or a switch in the corner, making sure that we swallowed it all down. Getting the medicine down was the hardest part.

1 teaspoon honey
1 teaspoon vinegar
1 teaspoon garlic powder or juice
1 teaspoon lemon juice

Momma would place all four items in a glass or cup and stir them together well. Since I didn't like the smell, I would have to swallow it down fast. After giving us any of her cold medicines, Momma would make us go straight to bed and cover up under her warm homemade quilts. We would have a good night's sleep. The next morning we would be ready to go to school or to work around the house.

Rusty Nails

Accidents happen all the time. Walking or running with bare feet puts you closer to problems. Stepping on a rusty nail or a sharp object hurts a lot, and on Daufuskie, no doctors were around to provide an antibiotic. Mad and hurting, you have to do something before it gets worse.

For us the cure was a piece of greasy fatback bacon, a penny, and something to tie it with. However, you first took a flat stick or board to beat the poison blood out from the place where the rusty nail went in. It is said that a rusty nail can cause blood poisoning and lockjaw if the wound is not treated properly. This is what worked for us at that time. Today we make sure we get to a doctor.

We used a piece of flat board to spank or beat the area around the puncture for about 2 to 3 minutes until the bleeding slowed. The blood that came out was said to be poisoned blood from the rusty nail. When we'd done that, we wiped or rinsed the area clean. Then we placed a piece of fatback over the area and placed a penny on top of the fatback. We tied a piece of clean cotton cloth around the penny and fatback on our foot and tried not to walk on it for about a day. To this day, I don't know how this works, but believing is as strong as anything.

Gas, Indigestion, Asthma

Pop said if you eat well, work hard, and have a good night's sleep, getting sick wouldn't have time to catch up with you. He said it's like keeping one step ahead of the things that may ail or hurt you. But in case we didn't get enough of the right things and got sick, the following remedy is one Momma and Pop believed in. Sometimes it was just a matter of taking it so that it could work.

One of the ingredients, "ether feather," was something Momma bought at the store; it came in a little blue box with a white swan on front. It looked like little crystal flakes. This remedy was used to help relieve gas pains in the chest and stomach. Ether feather's real name is asafetida, which we just couldn't pronounce. A good pharmacist will be able to find it for you even today.

1 teaspoon ether feather

1 pint gin

2–4 cloves garlic, mashed a little

We always had empty pint and half-pint bottles around to use as containers for homemade wine or medicines. Momma would put the ether feather in a pint of gin with the garlic, shake it well to combine the ingredients and let it sit for a couple of days. Momma would say, "Let it draw." Letting it sit made this remedy work better as it got stronger. My sisters and I were not allowed to take this without one of our parents' help. Momma would give us a teaspoon of the remedy with a glass of water or a piece of lemon to suck on as a chaser.

As a child I had asthma, and this remedy was given to me for that as well. Momma and others also believed that it was good for a child suffering from asthma to sleep with a cat breathing in his or her face. Momma said the cat would draw the asthma out as I slept. I outgrew my asthma. Whether the cat or the asafetida helped, I do not know.

Stomachache, Hookworm

Growing up with animals was lots of fun. But there was a time when we got hookworm from walking around with bare feet in the yard where they deposited their waste. Walking barefoot in the sand felt good to us, but hookworm was not a good thing, and Momma had to work on her remedy to help us get rid of the hookworms.

Hookworms are invisible to the human eye when entering the body. They are parasites that feed off the food in the body and grow, reproducing by the hundreds and causing the stomach to swell and ache. The host doesn't get nourishment from the food because of the worms eating it up. The more they reproduce, the more they cause the stomach to swell and become painful.

Many cases needed a doctor's care right away. But Momma tried to keep things under control by looking out for signs like sleepiness and fatigue, or our having a bigger appetite but not gaining weight. If she saw these signs, she knew it was time to get rid of those nasty worms that were slowing us down, and this is the fixin' she used to help kill the worms so we would pass them out later. Our bodies would begin to feel better, and Momma and Pop knew we would get our work done better.

1 teaspoon granulated sugar
2–3 drops turpentine

Momma would place the turpentine on top of the sugar in a spoon. We swallowed fast and sucked on a piece of lemon to help with the bad taste.

Diarrhea

Got to go fast? The human body has a way of letting you know when it needs help to make it feel better. For us, Pop and Momma believed that keeping it simple worked best. Momma would have us drink a cup of very strong brewed tea or eat a slice of dark brown or burnt toast. The trick was to digest either one, and then you would slow down.

Impetigo

As children we had a lot of impetigo, those bad sores that also left scars. All we knew at the time was what our parents and island folks believed. We always got up early in the morning while the grass was still wet with dew. We had to feed the chickens, hogs, dogs, and cats, and move the cows and horse to the field where they grazed before going to school. The early morning dew on the grass and bushes would coat our legs and feet. After a period it would cause us to break out with small, itchy bumps. We would scratch them, and the sores would break out all over our legs and feet. Momma would have us clean the sores with soap and water—they were very contagious. She would have us bathe in a tub of warm water using Octagon Soap, a lye soap, which would help them heal faster. Sometimes when Momma went to the mainland she would bring home peroxide to use as a wash for impetigo and other ailments as well.

We washed lots of things with Octagon Soap. Besides washing our bodies with it to get them good and clean, we also used Octagon Soap for things like our clothes, dishes, and floors. I've included a recipe for making lye soap at the end of this chapter.

Scrapes and Cuts

Living in the country, we got many scrapes and cuts. If someone got a scrape or a cut that was not bleeding seriously enough for a trip to the doctor across the water, we would reach up in a corner of the house or the porch and pull down a handful of spider web.

We would clean the injury with water, then dry it and place the spider web on the affected area, making sure it was covered; the spider web would stop the bleeding and help seal the injured area. A piece of cloth was then wrapped over the spider web and tied, and the excitement was over.

Spiders of many kinds made homes for themselves all over the corners of rooms in the house we lived in or outside around the front and back porches year-round. We never bothered them and they never bothered us; they would come and go freely. Pop always said, "If it ain't bothering you, you should not bother it." We believe they do the job they were put here to do; we weren't scared of them from a distance. We were taught that they were around for good reasons, but we believed that all spiders were poisonous, so we never played with them as pets.

Sore Throat, Strep Throat

Sometimes you get a sore throat when you least expect it. Your throat swells and gets very painful in a short time. It becomes inflamed, and it hurts to swallow; sometimes you run a fever. When this happened, Momma would have us gargle several times a day with warm salt water, with a squeeze of lemon if any was around. She would encourage us to swallow a little bit of the water, too. We were also given a piece of hard rock candy medicine when it was available; we would suck on it to help ease the pain.

Sore, Swollen Muscles

There were some home remedies that only the adults got to use. Momma and Pop let us know that we would have plenty of time later on to find out what aching bones and joints were all about.

We always had horse liniment around, whether it was for the horse or for our parents. We would rub down the horse or mule after it had had a hard day's work. This would help it feel better for work the following day.

Momma and Pop would use the same liniment for the aches and pains in their muscles.

If Pop and Momma had gotten swollen, sore muscles from all the work that they tried to get done in one day, they would have us go into the old field to pick some of the wide, soft leaves with a flannel-like feel on a plant called mullein. Some people called it deer tongue because they said it felt like the tongue of a deer.

Momma would make a hot compress and then wrap it around the sore area, leaving it on until it made her or Pop feel better. Mullein grew everywhere, even near our yard. "Go yondah and bring me da mullein plant, churn," Momma would demand for her aching leg. Momma had made sure we knew exactly what plant to look for, so we would run off and pick a big bunch for her.

Ringworm, "Wigworm"

Momma and Pop always told us that ringworm was catching. We got it a lot in our scalp (so we called it "wigworm") and sometimes over our bodies. Our cure for getting rid of it was right in the back yard. We would go to the fig tree, pop off a leaf, and a milky substance would come out. We would spread that on the spot and coat it from day to day, and it worked every time. When Momma braided our hair and we had it, she would part our hair and leave the affected area open so it could "catch air"; she would never braid over it. She said that the fresh air would heal it faster, and it did.

Earache

If there's one thing you don't want to have, it's an earache when the doctor is too far away. It hurt so badly sometimes when I was little that it would make me cry. And we didn't have much to help ease the pain. Momma and Pop knew that there was little to be done, but Momma would keep a bottle of medicine called "sweet oil" that she bought on the mainland. This was a medicine her parents had also used for their ears when they hurt. It came in a small brown bottle. You would put several drops into the ear that hurt and then place a piece of cotton in the ear to keep the oil in and the wind out. Keeping the ear closed off with cotton helped relieve the pressure that you felt.

Toothache, Tooth Pulling

Having a bad toothache can be one of the worst feelings imaginable. Not having a dentist around to help ease the pain wasn't a good thing. But at least Momma knew a way to help ease the pain, and to get what Momma needed we didn't have to go far—just out to the toothache tree that grew in the woods. We would cut off a small branch or chip off a small piece of bark, bring it back to the house, and boil it. When the tea was boiled and cooled, we would take a big mouthful and hold the liquid on the bad tooth until it helped ease the pain. Then we had to spit it out. Sometimes placing a small piece of the unboiled bark on the sore gum helped. Even though we called it the toothache tree, Momma said the real name of the tree is prickly ash (but some folks called it pickle ash) or devil stake.

I don't recommend that you use tobacco for anything, but we sometimes used it also to make a toothache feel better. A wet pinch of tobacco from a cigarette or a cigar placed on the gum of the bad tooth helped to make the bad pain ease up, giving some relief.

Pulling a tooth can be scary, whether the tooth is hanging by a fine thread or is down in the gum but needs to be removed. One day Pop thought that it was time to show us a quick and easy way to extract a loose tooth without knowing it was gone. You would first cut a piece of strong thread or string about two to four feet long. Tie one end to the loose tooth using a slipknot tie. Then tie the other end of the thread to a doorknob. Distract the person's attention, then quickly slam the door: out comes the tooth. After the tooth was pulled, you would rinse your mouth with warm salt water to help heal the sore gum—and then put the tooth under the pillow for the tooth fairy.

Gumball: Mouth Sores

Having a gumball in your mouth can be pretty painful from beginning to end. You don't hear much about gumballs these days. A gumball is an infected area on the lower or upper gum in the back of the mouth that starts out as a little ball and then swells up painfully. When a gumball occurs, there's very little you can do until it comes to a head or "ripens" (meaning the infected area is ready to burst). There was a method we used to help it get to that point a little more quickly and less painfully. Momma, like most other island natives in this situation, would scoop up a tablespoon of cool ash from the woodstove and place it in a bowl, mixing it with half that amount of salt. When the salt and ash were combined, she would take a pinch and lightly rub it over the gumball.

This was not easy to do without hurting, so she had to be gentle when she did it. In a day or so the gumball would come to a head; sometimes it would then burst on its own, but at other times it needed a little prick to open it up and let it drain. The pain would then lessen; we repeated putting the ashes and salt on the swollen gum as needed until it cleared up and stopped hurting.

High Blood Pressure

Spanish moss adds character to the trees all over Daufuskie Island. Visitors and natives alike see the moss hanging from the trees as beautiful. Not only was it plentiful when I was a child, it was also useful in many things that we did. Like many islanders, Pop and Momma believed in doing all sorts of things for comfort. During my parents' younger days, Spanish moss was used for stuffing mattresses and pillows. We fed our cows and horses the Spanish moss.

It was also said to be good for treating high blood pressure. If you put some green Spanish moss in your shoes, it would help bring down your blood pressure. They put in only enough so that they could still wear their shoes comfortably. They allowed the moss to stay in their shoes until it was dry, then removed it and repeated the process. Folks somehow knew when the green Spanish moss had helped lower their blood pressure.

I never understood how the Spanish moss helped, but it worked for island folks. It was their belief and nature's way. For them it worked, and that was all that mattered.

Pop was quick to remind us, "I fa know what fa do, cause all dem [doctors] want is ya money. It don't coss a dime to put dem moss in me shoe ta feel better." Most times there was a story behind the remedies, and Momma would join in and agree with Pop. Sometimes country folks had to do things the way country folks were taught to believe.

Pneumonia

Pneumonia was one sickness everyone tried to stay away from, but every once in a while, an islander would get it. Long before anyone would get sick Momma would fix up her cure as a precaution. It came from one of the very animals we raised. When a hog was killed, Momma would make sure she used every part of the hog possible for something. She would make sure we saved the black hog hoof. Sometimes she saved all the hooves, no matter what color they were, but there was something special about a black one. She would clean it and bake it in the oven. Then she would cool it, dry it, and break it up.

She would put it in a jar with some gin or homemade moonshine, add some fresh crushed garlic cloves, and let it sit for a week or more. When we had to drink this concoction, we just opened our mouths wide and swallowed it down. We did not dare spit out our medicine or say we did not want it.

Warts

A wart is a growth on top of the skin. Sometimes it can be a nuisance, but we knew how to remove it with a few strands of horsehair. We would pluck a few strands of hair from a horse's mane or tail, choose one, and tie it around the wart as tight as we could get it. Then we would slowly, slowly tighten the hair to a knot. The sharpness of the horsehair would cut the wart off safely, with hardly any bleeding. Some people are bleeders, and using the horsehair somehow worked even for them.

Hiccups

Sometimes it's the littlest thing that you believe in that matters the most. For example, when a baby on Daufuskie had hiccups, we would tear a very small piece of brown paper bag (about 1/4 inch or less), wet it, and place it on the forehead of the child. After it had been there for a while, the hiccups would go away. Another method we used was to take a broomstraw, break it evenly into two 1-inch pieces, and make a cross over the "mole"—the center soft spot in the hair, right in the middle of the head. We left it there until the hiccups went away.

Older children and adults would hold their breath and count to ten or swallow several chunks of dry bread or drink big gulps of water fast. The key is to trick the hiccup as you breathe. Older folks used to say that when a child gets the hiccups it means that he or she is growing.

Constipation

We ate a lot, but we did not eat enough of the right food. Momma and Pop would line us up every so often and give us a big dose of castor oil or cod-liver oil. It was nasty stuff, but it kept us regular.

Headaches

Having a bad headache can put everything on hold. Headaches can start at any time for anyone, whether you are young or old, sick or healthy. Allergies, stress, or specific medical problems can cause a headache.

Watching your diet and being kind to your body can help prevent headaches. But today, when they do occur, we have all sorts of painkillers to help. One way we used to help ease the pain without medication was to relax and elevate our feet. Sometimes a cup of warm soothing tea could help. Lying down for an hour or two sometimes helped. If a headache was caused by a bump on the head, we tried to see the doctor. All headaches hurt, and some are signs of serious problems, so it's better to see a doctor than to take chances.

Choking on a Fish Bone

Eating as many fish as we did, we sometimes got a bone or two stuck in our throats. We island folks learned how to eat a fish for its meat, not its bones, but, as Pop would say, even the best get caught off guard and make a mistake. Bread was more than just part of a meal for us when we needed to clear a fish bone caught crossways in our throats. Momma or Pop would have us first try to cough it up. If that didn't work, we would have to swallow a nice chunk of cornbread or light bread (store-bought bread). Most times, after a few tries at forcing the chunk of bread down, the fish bone would dislodge. A little sore throat was the result, but gargling with warm salt water took care of that.

HOME REMEDIES

Wetting the Bed

If Momma noticed us trying to bring in too much wood, she would remind us not to carry so much at one time. She believed that straining to carry too much would hurt our young backs and would make us have weak bladders, causing us to wet the bed nightly. Some kids are just born with weak bladders. Island folks believed that the cure for this was to drink water from a conch shell that had been boiled to remove the meat. As with a lot of these folk cures, whether it worked or not was all in your belief.

Ticks, Redbugs, Fleas, Bedbugs

Ticks and redbugs were bad during the hot summer months on Daufuskie, and if we went into the woods, we got them on us. Nine times out of ten they would hitchhike a ride back home with us or our animals. We spent a lot of time in the woods for both work and play. Sometimes we would not know they were biting into our flesh until they were halfway in. Momma knew we spent a lot of time in the woods, so she would have each one of us lie across her lap after a bath so that she could look over our body from head to toe. Even though Momma's eyes were good, she would sometimes miss the biting bug in our skin. My sisters and I would also take turns looking over each other's bodies.

Momma had her way of getting rid of the biting bugs. She would have us put a few drops of kerosene, bleach, or liniment on top of the bug. The bug would wiggle itself out.

Jumping fleas were treated the same way. There was no cure for bedbugs except to get rid of the mattress that was infested with them.

Old-Fashioned Lye Soap

Lye soap was a long-lasting soap, and we used it for many things in and around our house. We washed clothes, dishes, our bodies, the floors, and more with it. But as much as we used lye soap, we didn't make much of it.

Momma had more than her share to do without taking on that job. And we could buy Octagon Soap. The few times Momma made lye soap, we were at school. Here is the recipe as she remembers it.

  1 gallon leftover grease (not burned)
  4 gallons water, divided
  3 boxes Red Devil Lye

Strain the crumbs from the grease and place it in a large iron kettle or washtub. To start, add 2 gallons of water to the grease in the kettle; add the lye and boil for about 30 minutes, stirring constantly, until the lye eats up the grease (the mixture will become lighter and lighter). then add the other 2 gallons of water. Continue cooking, stirring constantly, until the mixture is the consistency of honey. Remove from heat and let cool in the pot for several days. Cut it out of the pot in the size and shape of your choice.

A Good Tip for the Kitchen: Burned Rice

Have you ever put rice on to cook and not turned the heat down enough—and the next thing you knew, you smelled burning rice? If the rice is so badly burned that it has browned on top and around the edge, just throw it away and start over. Otherwise, try this method to help you save the rice for dinner.

Remove the rice from the heat. Remove the lid from the pot; tear a piece of brown paper bag large enough to cover the opening and place it over the rice pot, then replace the lid. Turn the heat on low, let cook slowly and check often until the smell is just about gone. The brown bag will absorb the smell from the rice, and the bad, burned taste will be gone, too, so you can eat the rice (and no one else needs to know you burned it). The burned rice will still stick to the bottom of the pot, so be careful not to scrape any of it up when you serve the rice. If the smell of burned rice lingers in the air, see the next tip.

How to Get Rid of the Smell of Burned Food in Your House

A watched pot won't boil. But the minute you turn your attention to something else, it will not only boil but boil over. And it will surely make a mess or burn up a good dinner. Here is an easy, old-fashioned way to help eliminate the burned and smoky scent from your house and furniture without spending a bundle.

Combine equal parts water and distilled vinegar in a medium to large pot and let it boil. The steam from the boiling pot will fill the air, and the scent of the vinegar helps eliminate the smoky odor. It will get rid of the bad smell and leave a fresher scent.